Praise

EMBRACE YOUR MAGNIFICENCE

"Loving the essence of who you are is the key to true and lasting happiness. In *Embrace Your Magnificence*, Fabienne beautifully illustrates how to embrace your authentic worth and live an exceptional life."

—MARCI SHIMOFF,
professional speaker and #1 *New York Times* best-selling author of *Happy for No Reason, Love for No Reason,* and *Chicken Soup for the Woman's Soul*

"In her book, *Embrace Your Magnificence,* Fabienne opens her heart and her deep well of personal experience to provide you with great wisdom. If you are ready to stop wishing and whining and begin living the life of your dreams, let this book be your guide."

—ARIELLE FORD,
author of *The Soulmate Secret*

"You're here to live a life filled with passion, joy, and purpose. Fabienne's book shines a light on the way."

—JANET BRAY ATTWOOD,
transformational leader and co-author of the *New York Times* bestseller *The Passion Test*

"Truly transformational! Such a beautiful book with a beautiful message written by a beautiful woman. Fabienne carries the torch that shines a light on women everywhere! Read it . . . then pass it on to your own network of amazing women."

—SANDRA YANCEY,
founder and CEO eWomenNetwork, Inc.

The following words of praise for *Embrace Your Magnificence* are from a select group of students of The Client Attraction Business School™. These successful, strong women entrepreneurs are each on a journey of self-discovery that has allowed them, among countless others, to get out of their own way so they may live a richer, fuller, more abundant life they love.

"I was at a turning point in my life when I literally wished—out loud—for a mentor. Shortly thereafter I met and began to work with Fabienne Fredrickson. Know that as you are holding this book, you, too, have wished for Fabienne. And as you turn to the first page, you are courageously accepting her invitation to begin an incredible journey—a journey that will leave you forever changed. Through the heartbreaking yet triumphant stories so beautifully shared in her first book, *Embrace Your Magnificence*, Fabienne will become a gentle and omnipresent force in your life. Fabienne's words will give you permission to reevaluate the role you play in your life, to shed your self-limiting beliefs, and to set free your most paralyzing fears. Through her, you will step center stage into your own life. You will embrace your magnificence."

—Heather B. Habelka

"Two parts how-to and one part a personal retelling of her own life story, through *Embrace Your Magnificence* Fabienne Fredrickson provides the blueprint to a richer, more magnificent life. If you are feeling unworthy of love, afraid of rocking the boat, or just unsure of your next step, Fabienne will gently teach you the mind-set of playing a bigger game and then give you the strategies to face your fears, trust your intuition, discover what makes you uniquely you and share it with the world. This must-read book will serve as a life-changing guide for you in both your professional and personal life."

—Catherine Avery

"This is a book like no other I've ever read . . . a must read for every woman who's ever felt 'less than' or 'not good enough.' Having known Fabienne Fredrickson for years, I knew she was an incredible businesswoman and human being. In this book, she goes beyond. She reveals how all of us have felt at some point in our lives and does more than just tell her story . . . she relates it to all of us. This book gives you real strategies to not only survive but to thrive in your life—no matter what that looks like now, or how you want it to look in the future."

—Diane Conklin

"This is a book to keep, to read again and again. Fabienne Fredrickson lovingly shines the light into the dark pockets of our lives we may be ashamed of or afraid to see and discuss with openness and compassion. With courageous sharing from her own personal growth, humor, and an almost physical love for the reader, *Embrace Your Magnificence* unveils with each page the inner work and outer steps to shed the doubts, fears, and beliefs that hold us back from becoming our best selves.

"Clear a half day from your busy schedule and dive into this book. You won't be able to put it down. Listen to the whispers from each chapter as your truth becomes known to you and fall in love with your future."

—Kelly Azevedo

"When we need some help, it comes to us when we honor the voice of the one speaking. Fabienne's voice rings true for women of all ages and promises to be a letter to daughters everywhere. I'm honored to have heard her voice."

—Kathleen Mundy

"Reading *Embrace Your Magnificence* makes the reader feel as though she's sitting in Fabienne's kitchen, having a cup of tea with a sage, dear friend. Fabienne Fredrickson offers a window into the life of a transformed woman—and the narrative is enlivened with candid stories of moving from a pained past to manifesting an authentic, self-aware, and successful life. Through practical advice, exercises, and uninhibited honesty, Fabienne brings the basic but often elusive concept of loving oneself to an achievable goal—one illustrated by the candid and raw experiences of her own life transformation.

"Important concepts, from self-judgment to judging others, seeking approval, or facing the fears that hold us back, are offered without pretense. Fabienne lovingly pulls away the masks we wear to protect ourselves from the pain of old childhood 'stories.' Those stories infiltrate our lives and minds and get in the way of real personal triumph. Fabienne asks us to replace them with trust, honesty, intuition, and self-love.

"Women from tween to maturity who face life's biggest hurdles will benefit from studying the concepts and straightforward solutions Fabienne presents, allowing us to truly embrace ourselves for the unique people we are. Grab a cup of tea and begin the wonderful process of embracing your magnificence. You will see your life through new eyes forever after."

—Teri Goetz, CPC, MS, L.Ac.

"As I read Fabienne Fredrickson's book, *Embrace Your Magnificence,* I was often struck with the thought that although we are all unique, we are also the same. So many have similar struggles and experiences (to different degrees) through our lives that limit us and detrimentally change our beliefs about ourselves. Fabienne honestly shares her story in a way that is personal and compassionate. There are books that I read all the time by just opening the book and reading wherever it opens. *Embrace Your Magnificence* is one of those books. No matter where the book opens, there is a life lesson that is worth the time to reflect on, giving us permission to make different choices, believe in ourselves, and teach our children to be magnificent."

—Andrea Cinnamond

"In *Embrace Your Magnificence* Fabienne Fredrickson digs deep into her personal experiences to beautifully illustrate a journey up from the depths of low self-esteem. Even though the details may be different, as she writes early on in the book, 'my story is yours.' Fabienne truly wants the reader to deeply heal and grow in her own life—and she facilitates that through a generous helping of vulnerable sharing, exercises, affirmations, and the encouragement of ongoing self-reflection and self-care. I walked away from the book with the sense that my life will be profoundly changed for the better having experienced it.

"So many women desperately need the message in this book. I know I will be rereading and referencing the lessons in it for years to come."

—Christine Gallagher

"I was moved by the story Fabienne Fredrickson has lived and the information she shares in her book, *Embrace Your Magnificence.* Her journey was not a simple one, and yet she has truly embraced her own authentic brilliance. Her gifted storytelling style includes guidance on how to follow your own brilliance and helps you find the path to your life purpose. If you are looking for your right path, start by reading this book."

—Debra Vey Voda-Hamilton

"Fabienne Fredrickson's book, *Embrace Your Magnificence,* takes universal principles, such as self-acceptance, and makes them tangible for everyday consumption. It's the translation of 'woo-woo language' into common English with easy steps for taking action. She is open and frank in sharing her experience, making it okay to be human. Humility is a defining point of a master, and Fabienne is showing the way in this book."

—Luisa Rasiej

EMBRACE YOUR MAGNIFICENCE

$\mathcal{E}$MBRACE YOUR MAGNIFICENCE

Get Out of Your Own Way and Live a Richer, Fuller, More Abundant Life

FABIENNE FREDRICKSON

HAY HOUSE

Carlsbad, California • New York City • London • Sydney
Johannesburg • Vancouver • Hong Kong • New Delhi

First published and distributed in the United Kingdom by:
Hay House UK Ltd, Astley House, 33 Notting Hill Gate, London W11 3JQ
Tel: +44 (0)20 3675 2450; Fax: +44 (0)20 3675 2451
www.hayhouse.co.uk

Published and distributed in the United States of America by:
Hay House Inc., PO Box 5100, Carlsbad, CA 92018-5100
Tel: (1) 760 431 7695 or (800) 654 5126
Fax: (1) 760 431 6948 or (800) 650 5115
www.hayhouse.com

Published and distributed in Australia by:
Hay House Australia Ltd, 18/36 Ralph St, Alexandria NSW 2015
Tel: (61) 2 9669 4299; Fax: (61) 2 9669 4144
www.hayhouse.com.au

Published and distributed in the Republic of South Africa by:
Hay House SA (Pty) Ltd, PO Box 990, Witkoppen 2068
Tel/Fax: (27) 11 467 8904
www.hayhouse.co.za

Published and distributed in India by:
Hay House Publishers India, Muskaan Complex, Plot No.3, B-2,
Vasant Kunj, New Delhi 110 070
Tel: (91) 11 4176 1620; Fax: (91) 11 4176 1630
www.hayhouse.co.in

Distributed in Canada by:
Raincoast Books, 2440 Viking Way, Richmond, B.C. V6V 1N2
Tel: (1) 604 448 7100; Fax: (1) 604 270 7161; www.raincoast.com

Interior design: Pamela Homan

This book was previously published by Balboa Press (ISBN: 978-1-4525-7153-9).

The information given in this book should not be treated as a substitute
for professional medical advice; always consult a medical practitioner.
Any use of information in this book is at the reader's discretion and risk.
Neither the author nor the publisher can be held responsible for any
loss, claim or damage arising out of the use, or misuse, of the suggestions
made, the failure to take medical advice or for any material on third
party websites.

A catalogue record for this book is available from the British Library.

ISBN: 978-1-78180-418-6

Printed and bound in Great Britain by TJ International, Padstow, Cornwall.

To my children,
Claire, Luc, and Oliver,
for giving me the opportunity
to love myself unconditionally
when I became your mother.
You could have chosen
anyone to be your mother.
Thank you for choosing me.

To Derek, my husband, my partner,
my soul mate . . . my everything.
Thank you for choosing me.

CONTENTS

FOREWORD

Every once in awhile, a book comes along that really captures the essence of what it means to grow and become everything you are meant to become. In *Embrace Your Magnificence*, Fabienne has woven her own life lessons into a masterpiece that will help whoever reads it transform their own lives in such a compelling way that it should be required reading for every adult in the world.

The things that I love about this book and about Fabienne are her willingness to allow the reader into her mind and heart without holding anything back and the way she has taken many of her life's messes and turned them into her message. Through her pain, experiences, and personal triumphs, readers are engulfed in looking at their own lives and feeling hope and compassion for themselves. In addition, by following her path and prescription for life success, she makes it easy for anyone who is serious to duplicate her attitude and amazing lifestyle.

One of the things I loved most about this book is the authentic way in which all the lessons are revealed. They are shown in a way that is inclusive and warm, taking into consideration that each person has his or her own set of challenges and opportunities right now.

It's easy for someone to write a book telling you what you should do and why. It's another thing altogether to go on a personal journey with someone who opens up her heart and shares her deep life lessons with you so you can avoid pain and heartache.

I don't just recommend that you read this book. I urge you to study and apply each chapter as if your future success depends on it. I say this because it's easy to read a book. It's much more of a commitment to read and apply what's in a book.

I can let you in on a little secret right now. Fabienne stands out from the crowd because of her willingness to learn and apply her life lessons. Once she understands a lesson, she's off to the races, applying everything she has learned.

I know that Fabienne has invested hundreds of thousands of dollars in her own personal growth. You, my friends, have the benefit now to learn from and apply all the best lessons she has garnered in her life.

Read this book. Apply what you learn, and watch your life soar to heights you only dream of today.

John Assaraf,
New York Times best-selling author
of *The Answer* and *Having It All*

ACKNOWLEDGMENTS

To list everyone I'd like to thank for their roles in shaping my life, and therefore this book, would be an entire book in itself. There are countless people who had a part in this project, some of them listed below and many who know it in their hearts. Please know that the words that follow are only a miniscule representation of the vast gratitude that I feel for your contribution to my life and to this work.

To John Assaraf, for your friendship and guidance and for always stretching me to step into the next, bigger version of myself. The tears of resonance have paid off!

To Liz Dougherty, for your writing genius, your integrity, your love, and your willingness to walk this path with me. You felt the sacred intention of this project from day one, as if you had been divinely called to work on it. I am blessed to consider you my soul sister.

To Baeth Davis, for your unconditional love and friendship and for setting me on my path to living my life's purpose.

To Maria Gamb, for being the catalyst I needed to write this book.

To my team at ClientAttraction.com, for your dedication and willingness to give it your all, so that we may change people's lives on a daily basis. It is an honor and a true privilege to be on this journey with you.

To Bari Baumgardener, for being a great friend and always championing me.

To Blue Melnick, for seeing this book as just the first step of the Embrace Your Magnificence journey.

To Joan Falquet, for your most stunningly beautiful and inspirational illustrations.

To Joshua Rosenthal, for starting me on my path to personal growth, healing, and entrepreneurship.

To Lin Morel, for championing me and believing in my ability to be a force for good.

To the team at Balboa Press, for your guidance and expertise in making this dream of mine come true.

To my innumerable teachers, mentors, and healers, for giving me the guidance I've needed to get to this point in my life. I couldn't have done this without you.

To Louise Hay and Debbie Ford, for giving me permission to reveal my shadows and be my most authentic self.

To Oprah Winfrey, for being my source of inspiration, serving as a model of integrity and generosity personally and professionally, and being my mentor in absentia.

To my countless clients and students of the Client Attraction Business School, for consistently demanding that I show up as the biggest and best version of myself, with authenticity, integrity, and love. You are my tribe, and I love you.

To my family, especially my father. Papa, la confiance que tu m'as toujours montrée m'a aidée à croire que j'avais le pouvoir de faire ce que je désirais faire.

To my children, Claire, Luc, and Oliver, for beautifully and consistently reminding me that love is the most important thing in life.

To Derek, there are no words that would ever fully acknowledge the depth of what your presence in my life means to me. I admire you, I respect you, I honor you, and I love you.

PREFACE

My young daughter, Claire, is quietly sitting next to me at the dining room table, working on a school project.

Her delicate sensibility, innocence, and vulnerability are striking. Her intuitive nature and loving spirit are reminiscent of my own at that time in my life.

At her age, I'd already experienced my parents' divorce. I'd been raised between two cultures, feeling as if I didn't belong in either. Also at her age, and without knowing it, I would soon be taken from France by my mother to live permanently in the United States, leaving behind my father, my family, my friends, my school, and my culture to learn a new language and start a new way of being.

Even before moving, I'd never felt like I fit in with the majority of people I knew. I was somehow different from others and misunderstood by most. Once we moved, I was ostracized and bullied by other children. I really didn't belong. I had few friends, and sometimes I had none.

I felt unsafe in the world, lost, and abandoned. I couldn't make out who I was supposed to be, where I belonged, or why this was all happening to me. The pain inside was constant and gnawing.

As my loneliness and confusion grew, my self-esteem and self-worth spiraled downward. I felt that something was fundamentally wrong with me, that I wasn't good enough as a person, and that I had no one to talk to about it.

As a young adult, my life continued to be painful and lonely. I found it challenging to live in this world. I didn't have boundaries, and I had a tendency to attract "wounded" or abusive people. I was very sensitive, cried easily, and craved love and acceptance, often finding it in the wrong places, or, on the other end of the spectrum, I did whatever I could to numb myself.

As you'll read in the following pages, I allowed myself to be led off path. I said and did things that I still regret today. Most important, I fell out of love with who I was very early on. At the same time, I knew all along that I was here for a higher purpose, even if I was unsure what it was or how to fulfill it. It has been a steep climb up the self-esteem ladder ever since, and I've finally neared the top rung. I have embraced my magnificence and created a rich, full, abundant life I love.

Thinking about this makes me wonder how Claire would withstand similar childhood challenges, all in such a short period of time, with her temperament similar to mine. As I look into her eyes now, I want to cry. It's eerily as though I were looking into my own eyes at her age. I want to warn her, guide her, and share with her what I've learned along this bumpy road. I feel a great yearning to help her avoid some of the confusion and low self-worth I've felt so deeply.

It has occurred to me that having these feelings of not being good enough is a pervasive human condition. It affects boys and men, too, and yet I recognize this quiet desperation especially among women. Through countless years of working as a business mentor—and having worked on myself even longer—I have realized that many women actually feel "less than" and make decisions from a mind-set that they eventually regret. These women are everywhere. They don't know how to change direction and create lives they love.

The fire within me to protect my daughter from experiencing these feelings of inadequacy and to give her the tools for navigating her life eventually morphed into doing the same for the legions of other women (at every age) who feel "less than," who feel they somehow don't matter or aren't worthy. This is my calling, and it is my hope that this book answers this universal call.

INTRODUCTION

Years ago, in my home office overlooking the backyard, I had what I call a download from the universe:
"Fabienne, you must write a book and share your story
with other women struggling with the same issues of
not feeling good enough. Do it so they, too, can live happier, more meaningful lives." Problem is, I didn't know
how to write about it.

I'd been working with an intuitive, someone who
can channel my spirit guides, and when I asked her what
the book would be about, she simply said, "Write a letter
to Claire." I got chills.

As soon as I was told this, the entire outline of this
book was given to me. It was as if a force beyond me was
waiting for me to get this message out, that it needed to
be said, and that many, many women needed to hear it.

I sat down at my computer, and, within minutes, everything was on paper. Everything that I wanted to pass
on to my daughter, all my life lessons, and my journey
from low self-esteem to living a magnificent life were
now laid out. The shell was there. My job became to
flesh it out with my own journey of personal healing
and spiritual growth.

Writing this book began as a letter to Claire. I shared
with her all the important life lessons I've learned and
gave her the practical tools I've collected over the years

to navigate life. I told her to love herself unconditionally and to embrace how truly magnificent a woman she is, how deserving she is of all the abundance in the world.

And yet there is within me a sense of urgency bubbling up. I want to get this message out to women around the world—now, not later. I believe that when women realize how potent and magnificent they truly are, they will step up powerfully to shift their worlds. When a woman allows herself to see how glorious, brave, and brilliant she is, despite what she's endured previously, she will feel the courage to step out of her shell, stop playing small, and fully step into the potential of her own life purpose.

As a woman embraces how worthy she is, she plays a bigger game in all aspects of her life. When she heals the parts within that have been wounded and have held her back, she gets out of her own way and lives a richer, fuller, more abundant life. By doing so, she changes the lives of the people around her in ways and with a magnitude she will never really know. The ripple effects of this are endless.

This book is a culmination of all those hard-earned lessons in creating my own richer, fuller, more abundant life on all levels. It is a course in self-esteem as much as it is a path to healing, forgiveness, self-love, faith, and courage. It is a step-by-step process to achieving the abundance that naturally follows when you say yes to your own bigger purpose and journey.

You'll notice that I have allowed myself to be fairly vulnerable in these pages, to hold nothing back and be as transparent as I can be. Several times in writing these lessons, I was afraid to share as much of my own personal journey as I did. And yet in my work with clients over the years, the moments when I've been extraordinarily vulnerable and authentic are the times that my clients have created the biggest shifts in their own lives. They have built lives they love, while always striving to be even better versions of themselves.

So, despite my apprehension of "putting it all out there," I'm doing so with the hope that it may help you in your own journey. I hope it will serve a greater purpose and perhaps eventually create a ripple effect.

I share with you my formula for creating a life you love, despite any obstacles that seem insurmountable. In my case, it was low self-esteem, consistent self-criticism and self-loathing, abusive relationships, indulging in too much wine, and never feeling good enough to measure up. This process worked for me, and if you benefit from it, then I've done something good today.

Even if the details of your life are vastly different, my story is yours. And if you can be inspired to take action on the lessons in these pages to create the life, the career, the family, the income, the legacy, and the meaning you want in your life more easily and more quickly, then it will all have been worth it.

My intention is that you find something of value, a gem or two, a tool, or perhaps a way of thinking that will help you move forward past where you are currently—something that will lead you just a bit closer to where you know, deep in your heart, you belong. It is my hope that this process moves you to transform your view of yourself and stretches your vision of what you believe is possible for you.

I invite you to use these lessons as a way to move beyond your past and grow from your experiences. Through your own transformation and by embracing your magnificence, you will affect others around you in ways you may never fully understand. This is what changes the course of life.

Yes, you are that powerful . . .

As you read each page, allow yourself to see that you were created on purpose for a really big purpose.

This is a journey, and I have not yet reached my destination. I continue to apply the lessons that have brought me where I am today, along with new ones that will take me to the next stage of my life. The more I do this work, the more I become a role model for my daughter and my two extraordinary sons. I hope that you'll join me on this journey and bring others along with you so we can walk it together.

As you read each page and take in the stories and suggestions, let your heart guide you to think of other women in your life who would benefit from these lessons. Sisters, daughters, friends, or perhaps co-workers . . . invite them to go on this journey with us.

I believe that the core of this message is universal. It has the power and potential to change a person's life, and then to have a ripple effect into the lives of others.

I believe in you. I walk with you. I love you.

Chapter 1

Value, Honor, and Love Yourself

1. The truth about you

"To love oneself is the beginning of a life-long romance."

—OSCAR WILDE

Imagine that you are holding two babies, babies who come from different families and totally different cultures. Each will end up speaking a different language and looking quite different. But right now, look down at these two babies you are holding, one in each arm. They're looking up at you, gurgling, smiling, with their sweet little gazes sinking into your eyes. What you can feel from each baby is all the love that is available in the world.

When you're looking down at them, looking from one to the other, is there one who you feel deserves more love than the other? Is there one who is better and more deserving of warmth, nourishment, and hugs than the other? Is there one who is more worthy than the other? How does your heart answer these questions?

No matter what they look like, no matter where they come from or who they will eventually become, you know that neither baby is born more deserving than the other. Each has immense value and is just as worthy as the other. Both are deserving of the highest amount of love, compassion, and care.

This is true for all babies in the world. Pair up any two children born into drastically different circumstances, and each will still have unconditional worth.

And the same is true for you.

You were a baby once, and you had unconditional worth then. And you have unconditional worth now. This truth can never be taken away from you. There are no limitations or restrictions that can be put on your innate value. There are no conditions or exceptions that make this not true. The degree to which you deserve love and all the abundance in the world is unlimited.

You were made as a magnificent person who has and will always have unconditional worth. This cannot be disputed. You innately have great value, no matter what you've done, what's happened to you, or what others have said or done to you. It is your birthright.

The fact that you are a good person can never be taken away from you. All people are good at the core. Even "bad" people are good at the core. They've just chosen behaviors and actions that aren't true to their natures. Whenever someone is judged, he is judged for his behaviors, not his core value. Behaviors can be poor or even awful, but the person cannot be. Luckily, behaviors can be changed in an instant.

If you peel away all your experiences, all the external circumstances, and get back down to the core of who you are as a person, back to that baby you once were, you realize that you, in fact, are that baby now, just grown up. You are all love, and you are all-deserving.

Great things are in store for you. Realize and live the fact that you have unconditional, unquestionable worth.

2. The icing does not make the cake

"Worth doesn't have to be earned or proved.
It already exists. Just recognize, accept, and appreciate it."

—GLENN SCHIRALDI

At the core, no person is better than another. Yet it's so easy to measure another person as more worthy than we are, based on what we see on the outside. We've been led to believe that someone who has more money, someone who is considered more beautiful, someone who achieves more than we do, or someone who performs better at a certain task is a better person. We define ourselves and others based on social status, possessions, looks, and weight.

I have always been fascinated by why there are so many women in the United States who dye their hair blonde. If you look around a restaurant, a shopping mall, in magazines, and on TV, you'll notice that a majority of women choose blonde as their hair color. I, too, have always wanted my already blonde hair to be even lighter and blonder. And, no, I don't believe it's because "blondes have more fun." I believe that we've had it burned into our brains that to be desirable, to be worthy, we need to look a certain way: like Barbie.

I have told my children repeatedly, especially my daughter, that Barbie is not real and that no one can look like that naturally: bleached-blonde hair, an abnormally small waist, and legs that are longer than the rest of her. Let's not mention her thighs or flawless face. And yet because we've spent countless hours of playtime focusing on Barbie's looks and proportions, we have convinced ourselves that if we do not look like that, something is fundamentally wrong with us.

I still have fond memories of playing with my Barbie, but I'm also very aware of how this doll has worked into our subconscious conditioning. Barbie affects how we view external things as the basis for self-worth and value.

When I moved to the United States from France at the age of ten, I didn't speak English, I didn't look the way the other kids looked, I didn't dress like they did, and I didn't fit in. After observing my surroundings, I came to believe that if I could just change my exterior (the clothes I wore), I would be worthy of their attention and inclusion. So I begged my mother to take me to Kmart and buy a few very specific shirts, pants, and shoes that I thought were hideous, just so I could fit in. At that moment, I created a meaning about myself that I wasn't good enough unless I looked a certain way or had a certain possession.

What I didn't realize until years later is that, no matter what you do to your outside, your core is the same. No icing you slather on top of it can make you a better person or a lesser person. We are all equal in worth—no matter who we are and no matter what the externals say. Money doesn't change that—neither do looks, clothes, cars, social status, achievements, possessions, performance, or belonging to an exclusive group. Having these doesn't make you better than someone else, and not having them doesn't make you less than anyone else, despite what you may have experienced.

Thinking otherwise is the great lie, and it's insidious. It causes greed and pompous pride, and, most especially, it causes the deep pain of believing we are not enough. Believing the great lie is so deeply ingrained in our culture that going against it seems like a losing battle.

Just remember, we are children of the same Creator. In that, we are equal. Just as a child has part of her mother in her, your Creator is part of you, and you are part of your Creator. Since God uses only the best "materials" for His creations, then by default you are all love, as is everyone else. One may have less money; one may have a newer car; one may have smaller breasts; another may be better at sports. Some may have a different color skin, others may have a more desirable job, and yet others may have chosen a different path or set of behaviors than you would have. But in the end, we are all the same in worth.

Because no one is better than you and you are not better than anyone, you must treat people as your equals. Treat people as your own sisters or brothers, just as you would want to be treated: with respect, love, compassion, and forgiveness. When you do this, you tear down the walls that keep you separated. You begin to feel really, really good about yourself.

3. An unlikely compass

*"A rejection is nothing more than a
necessary step in the pursuit of success."*

—BO BENNETT

One of the greatest fears people experience is the fear of rejection. That's because there are few things that hurt as much as rejection. We create meanings about our worth based on incidents in which we've been rejected. These meanings then help shape our self-image, which dictates the decisions we make in our lives.

It's very easy to believe that when someone rejects you, whether it's in love, friendship, family, work, or otherwise, it's because something is wrong with you. Anyone and everyone can be rejected, no matter who they are. Your worth stays the same even when someone rejects you.

If someone rejects you, it doesn't diminish your innate value because it doesn't affect your soul. It affects your ego, which loves to blame and thrives on making you feel like a victim. But your soul stays perfectly intact. The essence of who you are, the core of you, doesn't change, and neither does your worth. The unconditional worth you had at birth is still the same. Whether you are included or excluded by someone doesn't change that.

Rejection hurts when we internalize it. When we do this, we allow someone else's actions and opinions to shape how we feel about ourselves. We then create a belief that the person who has rejected us is better. Conversely, we start to believe we are somehow unworthy.

Yes, those who've rejected you may have had their reasons or rationales for doing so. Those reasons don't have to be about you specifically, and they don't mean anything about you as a person. In fact, the meanings you created about yourself based on rejection are actually not true. The key is not to internalize it and not to feed the ego.

I will explain how to do this, but first, let me share this example.

When my mother died suddenly while I was in college, I began staying out late to drown my sorrows. I didn't show up for classes, and I quickly started failing. I felt lost and wanted badly to have direction in my life. I desperately looked for an anchor to get me grounded. I wanted something to belong to that would make me feel significant, like I mattered.

I applied for the position of social chair of my sorority. Being a social person, I thought that I would be great at it. The day we were to vote on the members of the new board, we all assembled in the sorority meeting room, and I was anxious. After several board positions were voted on, it was time to elect the social chair. The president asked the applicants to raise their hands, and, once acknowledged, we were asked to leave the room while the other members discussed the applicants and took a vote.

I came back into the room and learned that I hadn't made it. So when the next position was offered, I raised my hand. Again, I left the room while the decision was being made. And, again, I wasn't selected.

I started to feel embarrassed, but because I so desperately wanted to have something significant in my life, I raised my hand to apply for the next position. Once again, I was not chosen. This happened again and again until the entire board was filled.

Each time another name was called, my heart sank to my stomach. That day, it felt as if I died several deaths, one after the other. I felt like the whole room, the whole sorority, and the whole world were against me. I couldn't believe they hadn't taken pity on me, especially after having applied so many times. Especially since my mother had just died. I wanted them to throw me a bone, but, instead, it was the ultimate rejection.

I left that room crushed, embarrassed, and humiliated, having lost every ounce of confidence that I had. I felt worthless, unloved, and unlovable.

That night, I cried and cried into my pillow, feeling like a victim, blaming them, and hating every single one of them. I wanted to punish them. After I dried my tears, I decided that I was going to leave the sorority, drop out of college, and move back to France to be with my father. So I did.

It wasn't until close to 20 years later that I realized what had actually happened in that room. I created an image of myself as unworthy and unlovable, based on that experience. Looking back now, I will admit that my opponents had prepared elaborate presentations and detailed how they would use the social chair position to create a better year, and I hadn't prepared anything. I didn't have a plan. I just showed up and expected to win based on my personality.

But I never thought deeply enough about why I hadn't gotten any of the positions I had applied for. Then it dawned on me that while I was blaming them for humiliating me, abandoning me, and rejecting me, they had had no choice. To represent the sorority in a leadership position, one was required to have a good grade point average. I had failed at least one class, and my GPA was very low. The sorority couldn't help me. Because the voting process and discussion were top secret, I didn't realize that until much later.

What I see now is that leaving college was one of the best things that could have happened to me. I don't advocate that for everyone, but for my self-esteem and my evolution, it was important that I leave and start my career. It was important for me to move in with my father so that I could feel grounded. It was time that I started my life. If I'd stayed in school, I would have delayed that process for another two years, probably failing many other classes.

There was a reason for the sorority incident, but it wasn't until I looked past my ego and humiliation that I saw the blessing in it. Though it felt like I had died a thousand deaths, it was a divine, defining moment, and it was in my long-term best interest.

See the bigger picture in rejection. If someone rejects you, it's because you're just not meant to be in that situation, no matter how much you want it. In fact, if I look back on every rejection I have endured in my life, unequivocally, each was there as a compass to take me in a different direction that would bring me back to my soul's path. Each rejection was a correction. When I was going off track in my soul's journey, the rejection was a realignment toward what was best for me.

We all have things that happen to us that don't make us feel good about ourselves. But the difference between people who are happy and healthy and those who are miserable and bitter is that happy people don't internalize or create a meaning about themselves based on a particular rejection.

It's best to look at rejection as an opportunity for something else, something better, waiting just around the corner.

Think of a new door opening after an old door has been slammed in your face. Even though rejection feels like a small death, there is a reason for it. While this door is being closed to you, there is a much better set of circumstances awaiting you behind the next door. You must keep going.

Resist the temptation to blame or hate the person who rejected you, even if he or she wasn't nice about it. Find a way to wish that person well instead. You may not realize it in the moment, but that person is actually an angel in disguise, leading you in the right direction by putting an end to the path you were on.

See it as a divine redirection. Don't try to change their minds; likely they will not change. It's best to simply accept the decision and then move on.

4. Sticks and stones

"Sticks and stones may break my bones, but words will make me go in a corner and cry by myself for hours."

—ERIC IDLE

If you're anything like me, at some point in your life, you based your opinion of yourself on things that other people said to you or about you. Whether they were being nice or not, the problem is that nothing they said is accurate. Everyone else, even those who are closest to you, filters their views of you through their own perceptions, experiences, prejudices, life lessons, beliefs about life, and other factors.

This means that whatever someone thinks of you is not true. Even if others think they know you, they actually do not. Yes, that goes for your closest family members, too. They think they know you, but they're only seeing you through their own masks of perception, something that they don't have the ability to take off. So, if someone calls you something, it's really only his or her perception of who you are. It will never be true.

I remember trying to get out of the subway in New York City many years ago and bumping into a woman. I excused myself but got a nasty look from her. Then she called out to me, "White bitch!" with all the venom she could muster. I was stunned. Did she really think it was deliberate? Am I a bitch?

It really struck me, and I have remembered it ever since. I kept asking myself quietly, "How does a person think she can size you up in just a brief encounter, and think and say something so demeaning? Can anyone really know who you are and what you are made of? If she did, would she still consider me a white bitch?"

Yes, I can be bitchy, especially if I'm short on sleep—who isn't? But can anyone really know you, truly, when they don't live in your body and your thoughts and your feelings?

I thought about this further, and I realized that perhaps this woman had the perspective that anyone who is female and Caucasian must be a bitch. And if an encounter occurred that didn't feel right to her, then that encounter must have been premeditated. That may have been her view of life, and looking through that cloudy lens, she found example after example to prove her point and substantiate her belief system, even if her character assessment was based on a passing moment.

In junior high school, I made the dreaded mistake of admitting to the girls on the school bus that I'd once had lice. They were talking about it, making fun of someone, and I said, "What's the big deal about lice? I've had it. Doesn't everybody get it once in their life?"

I was immediately ostracized. The girl sitting next to me on the bus screamed, "Ewww!" and frantically moved to another seat, as did all the other girls sitting in my immediate vicinity.

From that day forward, notes were passed about me in class. Gum was put in my hair. I lost all my friends. When I sat down in the cafeteria for lunch, the minute my tray touched the table, everyone who was sitting at that table picked up their trays and moved to another table. I was bullied constantly, didn't have friends for many years, and endured a great deal of shame. Daily, I experienced unending humiliation and countless little deaths, just from one thing that I'd said.

(As a side note, I will never forget a particular group of girls who had also been ostracized in their own way for how they looked. They allowed me to sit at their table and never got up. Because they felt my pain, they accepted me in their own way, and I will forever be deeply grateful for their compassion and charity. To this day, when I see someone who resembles any member of that group of girls who allowed me to have lunch with them, I cannot help but feel the strongest of bonds and sisterhood.)

Sometimes your own family members and friends think they know you, based on a limited collage of past experiences they've witnessed. But they only know a part of you. It's easy to make a character assessment based on patchwork moments, but they never get to see the whole of you. So any opinion they have is skewed and flawed. And if you base your self-acceptance and self-esteem on flawed information, you will be mistaken, too.

The only opinion that matters about you is your own. The only person who truly knows you is you, because no one else lives with you 24/7, in every waking moment and with every thought and emotion. You may be tempted to create ideas of who you are in the world based on the things others say about you. Just remember that others are coming from their own experiences; they have their own fears and judgments and their own upbringings. What may be accurate for them is not valid for you.

The good news is that you create your opinion about yourself. It's a choice. You and only you decide if you feel that you are a good person (even though you always innately are good inside). The minute you make the decision that you are indeed a valuable person, then no matter what others say about you, you become that good person in your own eyes. That's when you begin to love yourself unconditionally. In turn, that is precisely when the opinion of others won't matter to you.

The moment you decide you love yourself is the moment you begin to love yourself.

5. An alternate reality

"What we can change is our perceptions, which have the effect of changing everything."

—DONNA QUESADA

I have experienced many things in my life that I didn't perceive as being "good." Because of my involvement in these situations, whether I was an active participant or someone on the receiving end, I created a meaning about myself as not being a "good" person, or "not good enough." It took me 40 years to realize that how you view any experience in your life is based on a perception that you created based on what you observed (or thought you observed) about that particular situation.

Once you've perceived an experience in a certain way, you create a meaning about who you are based on what you thought you observed, even if it's not true or accurate. The thing is, nothing is ever black or white about life. There are shades of gray in every situation. No experience is one-dimensional because life itself is not one-dimensional. There are many sides and perceptions to every story. Many different things are at play that can be observed, and therefore there are many different perceptions that can be created.

If your perception about an event makes you feel bad about yourself, it is probably one-dimensional. If you were to be shown all the different sides to the story, you might come to understand that the original meaning you created was not entirely valid.

This means your perception about something can be changed within seconds through something called reframing.

Let me give you an example. When I was a teenager, there was a boy I liked and wanted to spend more time with, but I wasn't sure if he liked me back. One day, I approached him at a gathering and tried to talk to him several times. He clearly was not interested. I felt crushed and rejected, and I immediately created a meaning about my worth based on this. I decided right at that moment that I was not pretty enough, not popular enough, not desirable enough—just not good enough all around.

That one event (along with several others that followed) affected me for years. In addition to creating a flawed judgment about myself, I also created a meaning about rejection: that when you approach someone who hasn't approached you first, you will always be rejected. Always. For the majority of my life, I subconsciously believed this, which affected many areas of my life. I also created a fear of rejection that followed me into adulthood, affecting my ability to go for what I wanted. In fact, it ultimately affected my income when I began a career in advertising sales.

Yes, one incident at age 15 or so was still affecting me many years later. Recently, though, I tried to see that perhaps there was nothing wrong with me in this instance. Perhaps I hadn't been reading the situation properly. Maybe there were things about him that I didn't know.

In fact, there are dozens, if not hundreds, of possible other scenarios. Perhaps that boy's girlfriend was there, too, and he didn't want to be seen talking to any other girl. Perhaps he liked me but was painfully shy and socially uncomfortable. Perhaps his parents were moving and he didn't want to start something new, knowing he'd have to leave soon. Perhaps he was gay and I didn't know it. There might have been any number of other reasons for what happened.

Sometimes we are rejected because we are not what the other person wants, without it being about us. The key here is that I don't know what I don't know about what happened then, and I never will.

But, even not really knowing what happened, I created a meaning about myself based on too little information. I assumed that something was wrong with me instead of thinking perhaps something was happening on his end. And so it stuck with me until I reframed the situation.

Reframing is really about acknowledging that there are several equally correct ways of looking at every situation. Yes, all can be correct, with the emphasis on the fact that there is more than one truth about any situation. Reframing is one of the most powerful techniques you can use to change the quality of your life instantly.

Answering these questions can help you begin to reframe any situation:

- What happened? (Just the facts, not the interpretations.)

- What was my interpretation of the situation? (Beyond the facts, now assumptions.)

- What meaning did I create about myself based on these assumptions?

- What else could have happened instead of what I think happened? What are some different scenarios that could have happened or different ways of looking at the situation?

- Based on these different ideas, is the meaning I therefore created about myself absolutely, positively true?

- Could my assumption or the meaning I created about myself possibly be false or flawed? Could it be disproved based on this new way of looking at the event?

When I tried to reframe my perceptions of what had happened in several instances in my life, it changed how I felt about myself within minutes. This is a powerful way of going from feeling like something's wrong with you to feeling completely neutral about it, thereby giving you some relief.

By reframing your experience in this way, by creating alternate scenarios to replace the (most likely) flawed one you originally created, you can make the situation be not about you anymore. Accept what you can about what happened and be freed from the false beliefs about yourself. If the story is reframed, then there is no meaning to be created, no new definition of what happened. The whole thing is null and void.

A particular event cannot make you a bad person. What makes you feel bad is what you actually say to yourself, based on a belief you created about yourself at the time of the event. In the end, you have a choice in how you perceive anything that's happened to you in your life. Which means you can have a choice in creating the meaning around a particular situation and what that situation means about you.

You are the author of your life. You create the story, and you can also rewrite it.

6. Toxic waste

"You have the right to quit Toxic People. (They're contagious.)"

—DR. SUNWOLF

17

Life is meant to feel good a majority of the time. It's true that not all moments are good moments, but when you spend time with people who don't make you feel good, you increase the moments you don't enjoy. If you continually feel bad about yourself when you spend time with a particular person or group of people, it's time to stop spending time with them.

When I was younger, I spent a lot of time with a close group of girlfriends. I thought we were the ultimate best friends. For many years, we did everything together. I was sold on the idea that I belonged to this close-knit group, especially after not having friends for so many years as a child. We had great times, but if I'm honest with myself, I didn't feel good around them all the time. I felt criticized, made fun of, and not always safe. And yet I thought that without them, I had nothing; I would be nothing. Until they started falling away from my life.

Little by little, for many reasons and under many circumstances, these friends no longer held a prominent place in my day-to-day life. They were replaced by people with whom I felt safer, who were softer and more compassionate. For the first time in a really long time, I began liking myself more. Without the constant little jabs, I started honoring myself more. And the more time I spent away from them, the more room there was for self-love.

You are not obligated to spend time with anyone you don't enjoy being with, even if others say you are or even if you think you are. Surround yourself with people who make you feel good about yourself when you're with them. Stop spending time with the others, or at least reduce the amount of time you spend with them.

After a while, let them know you prefer to spend more time by yourself. This will sometimes cause friction—in some instances, big friction—but there comes a time in your life, hopefully sooner rather than later, when you must honor who you are and who you spend your time with.

Please understand that I'm not talking about only surrounding yourself with people who are nice only because they want something from you. That's inauthentic. It's possible to be in a healthy relationship even when there are sometimes disagreements. But you should never spend your time with people who continually put you down, even if they don't realize they're doing it. (Deep down, they do realize it.)

If you consistently question your value when you're around a particular person or group of people, then you can stop spending time with them. Remember, you have innate value and unconditional worth. No one can take that away from you.

Gauge how you feel when you're walking away from time spent with a colleague, friend, group, or even family member. If the feeling you have afterward is one you don't want to experience again and again, then it's time to stop spending time with those people.

Toxic people have to go.

7. Love is . . .

"People who love you don't treat you badly. Love doesn't hurt. It's supposed to feel good."

—Oprah Winfrey

Based on everything that had happened to me through my teenage years, I had continual and profoundly low self-esteem that led me straight into abusive relationships. In fact, my very first relationship in high school lasted close to two years, and it was as abusive as anything I've experienced. There was mental abuse, physical abuse, verbal abuse, and lots of cheating. When the relationship was good, it felt great, as if I was on cloud nine; when it was bad and we mistreated each other, it felt as if I was living in hell and he was the Devil.

We broke up so many times . . . after the cheating, after the constant arguments, after he punched me in the stomach. And yet each time, I went back to him thinking he was the love of my life. I don't blame him as a person, nor do I blame a second abusive relationship that followed. I am very clear that I agreed to be in these relationships. I stayed in them, and I went against the advice of my mother and friends, against my better judgment and intuition. Even his mother took me aside one day and suggested I go to therapy. Instead of listening to her advice, I chose to be offended that she would suggest that for me instead of for him.

I was desperately looking for love, looking for some semblance of self-worth. I wanted to believe that I was lovable. At that point, I simply didn't believe that I deserved any better. I also despised being alone. When I was alone, my self-loathing had a chance to speak up.

Real love isn't a fairy tale. There will be some bumps in the road. But real love doesn't make you question your worth or who you are as a person. It doesn't affect your self-esteem negatively. If the "love" you have now does that, then it's not love. If it hurts continually and chronically, either emotionally, physically, or mentally, then it's not love.

My husband, Derek, has shown me that real love feels really good. It feels safe and nurturing. He has shown me that love goes hand in hand with respect, with admiration, with honor, and with tender care. The more you love and honor yourself, the more you will not tolerate anyone else betraying you, disrespecting you, or treating you badly. Anything other than respect, admiration, honor, and tenderness is not love.

There is no good enough reason for abuse of any kind. Nothing you could ever say or do is a good enough rationale for someone to strike you or violate you in any way.

In my parenting, I have at times asked my children to give me a reason for having lashed out or hit their siblings. "Why did you hit your brother?" I caught myself waiting for the answer, as if the answer would somehow justify the outburst. And then it washed over me. There is never a good enough excuse for someone to abuse you—physically, mentally, verbally, sexually, or otherwise.

When I was younger, I assumed that the reason I was being abused was that there was something wrong with me. I thought I didn't deserve anything better. But here's what's clear to me now: nothing you can ever say or do is a good enough excuse for someone to take advantage of you or to treat you badly. You are worth so much more than that. Don't let them do it. Listen to that little voice inside that's telling you to walk away from it. Say, "No more," and mean it. Walk away. Tell someone. Get help. Just get away.

8. Oh no, you don't

"The way you treat yourself sets the standard for others."

—Dr. Sonya Friedman

You are responsible for how people treat you in life, whether this sounds like something you're used to hearing or not. You were probably taught that when something happens to you, you are the victim and someone took advantage of you or dishonored you. But you must understand that it is partially (even in a small part) your responsibility when something happens repeatedly to you. Why?

People treat you the way that you train them to treat you, whether you're doing it consciously or not. If you condone the hurtful way people treat you the first time they do it, and you accept their behavior or continue to see them, it's like giving them permission to do this again and again. They will continue to treat you that way until you stop them or leave.

The way to teach people how to treat you in a way that feels good is to actually get clear on how you want to be treated in your life . . . and then write it all down, like a code of honor, but with yourself. Very few people ever write down how they want to be treated by others, what's acceptable and what's not. As a result, they let their interactions with others become silent approval.

Instead, you must be really clear on what standards you have for yourself and all your relationships, whether they are personal, intimate, professional, or family relationships.

This list of standards becomes a list of rules that you follow and that you make sure everyone else in your life follows. Once these standards have been defined, everyone will be on the same page about what's acceptable and what's not. Most important, this process allows you to set rules about how you want to live your life.

This list is actually more for you than anyone else. Once you get clear on your own standards for how you want to be treated (and how you don't want to be treated), it's much easier to enforce.

What goes on the list? Behaviors that you find acceptable. Behaviors that you find unacceptable. How you want to be treated. Some examples may be not being physically abused and not being verbally abused. Also take into account behaviors that aren't considered every day. The beginning of such a list might include rules such as these:

It is not acceptable to hit me.

It is not acceptable to shout at me.

It is not acceptable to cheat on me.

It is not acceptable to make fun of me or belittle me.

It is not acceptable to swear at me or call me names.

It is not acceptable to lie to me.

It is not acceptable to steal from me.

It is not acceptable to consistently be late and keep me waiting for a long time.

It is not acceptable to not keep your word to me.

Some of these might seem to be commonly accepted standards. Yet you'd be surprised to know how many people allow themselves to be taken advantage of again and again because they don't have these standards in their lives, even as grown adults. Possibly you are one of them. This especially occurs with someone close or a family member. We let our boundaries slip with those people.

Going further, you could include rules such as these:

It is not acceptable for me to be the only one cleaning up around the house.

It is not acceptable for my mother to call me several times a day while I'm at work.

It is not acceptable to pay me late or to not pay me back.

It is not acceptable to continually back out of plans at the last minute.

It is not acceptable to not return something you borrowed.

It is not acceptable to boss me around.

It is not acceptable for my spouse to continually forget my birthday or our anniversary.

It is not acceptable for my spouse to continually spend a full day golfing each weekend when I don't have a full day off to do what I want to do.

I didn't have many standards for myself earlier in my life. I allowed people to push me around, shout at me, deliberately make me cry, cheat on me, belittle me, mentally abuse me, lie to me, steal from me, and consistently make me wait, among many other things. Because I hadn't set any rules, I lived my life according to what others wanted, not what I wanted.

Each time something happened, I was confused as to why it was happening. I thought I deserved it, that somehow this was my fate. When these things happened, I continued to let them happen because I didn't understand that I could have standards, that I deserved to have standards, and that I could communicate to others how I wanted to be treated.

The minute you make your own list of standards is the minute your life starts getting better. The higher the standards you have in your life, the better your life will be. In the end, I came to love myself enough to set standards for my life and for those who are in my life. Or perhaps it was because I began to set these standards that I came to love myself. Which came first, the chicken or the egg?

If you'd like the list of standards as a reminder, you can download a copy at www.EmbraceYourMagnificence .com/resources.

9. Let 'em know where you stand

*"I wish you were a mind-reader. I want you to know
everything but I don't want to have to tell you."*

—LISA KLEYPAS

When you're clear on the standards you want to set for yourself and your life, you strengthen your understanding of what is acceptable behavior toward you and what isn't. But you can't assume that others will read your mind. Having standards listed on a piece of paper won't do any good unless you set strong boundaries and then enforce them.

Setting a boundary is like setting up a rule. First, you've got to be clear on what the rule is. Then the rule needs to be communicated. Otherwise, you're the only one working with the rule. This makes all the difference.

Communicating a standard is something that may happen before, during, or after an incident—preferably before. Once you've written your standards list and feel good about it, make a note next to each standard. Write down who in your life currently behaves in a way that goes against your standard.

For example:

I will no longer be the only one cleaning up around the house. (spouse, kids)

I will no longer allow someone to pay me late. (client X)

I will no longer allow someone to borrow money and not pay it back. (friend Y)

Now that you're more conscious of who specifically crosses the standards you have for yourself, it's important to communicate your new boundaries to those involved. The most successful way to communicate these is to choose a time when there is no flare-up or discord, when things are good, and then to phrase the new boundary as a request.

Making a request is a combination of being polite, respectful, and assertive at the same time, which improves communication. Instead of demanding, blaming, complaining, or muttering something under your breath in a passive-aggressive way, it is more successful to approach the subject by making a polite request.

It can be as simple as that, or it can involve a longer explanation if there are more complexities. But if you start with a polite request, you've officially set up a boundary with someone and, most important, with yourself. For example:

> **Complaining:** "Why don't we ever do what I want to do?"

> **Making a request:** "John, I'd like to make a request. I'd like to begin switching off what we do in the evenings. One night we do what you want to do, and the next night we do what I'd like to do. Would you be open to doing that? Would that be fair?"

> **Demanding:** "Chris, I hate it when you do that. Don't ever do it again!"

> **Making a request:** "Chris, I'd like to make a request. It doesn't feel good when you (insert what you'd like to have changed). Going forward, I'd like to request that you not do that anymore."

> **Passive-aggressive muttering:** "Why am I always the one cleaning up around everyone else in this house?"

> **Making a request:** "I'm holding this family meeting because I'd like to make a request. I often find myself cleaning up after other members of this family, and it doesn't feel good. I'd like to request that when you leave the table, you bring your dishes to the sink with you. I'd also like to request that you not leave your shoes in

the front hall and put them directly into your room. This is about all of us pitching in together to keep this house neat. Is that fair? Would you be willing to do that with me?"

Blaming: "Mom, I can't get any work done if you call me five times a day! Can you just stop calling me so much?"

Making a request: "Mom, I know that because I work from home, it may seem like I have a lot of free time on my hands to talk during the day. To be honest, nothing could be further from the truth. Because I'm responsible for making my own money, I've got to focus on my work during the day. I know you love me and you want me to be successful, and this is why I'd like to make a request. Instead of us speaking several times during the day while I should be focusing on getting more clients, would you be open to us talking after six o'clock in the evenings instead? Would you be willing to do that, so we can talk more freely and I can be totally focused on you?"

Notice how you would react if someone said the first version to you in each scenario. Would you feel attacked? Blamed? And, if so, would you pay attention to the demand or complaint? Probably not as much as you would to the request that follows.

You may even want to create some house rules and place them in a visible place, so that everyone is aware of the new standard of "how we do things around here" and what's expected of them. This could be a chart taped on the fridge and communicated during a weekly or monthly family meeting.

You can also create something similar for visiting guests. We often entertain our friends and family for weekends at our ski house. Here's how we request that they help out:

Fredrickson Ski House Details and Preferences
(none of these are obligatory, yet they are most appreciated)

As you can imagine, hosting a whole lot of fun friends over the winter season involves lots of behind-the-scenes organization and preparation. We'd love your help with the following, so as to make it fun for everyone involved, including us.

We've realized that tidiness really is next to godliness. Let's all agree to keep the main areas free of personal stuff if at all possible (kitchen, living room). We tend to keep our stuff in our own bedrooms.

Feel free to put dishes straight into the dishwasher. Here's something you may not know: one of Fabienne's least favorite things to do is unload the dishwasher several times a weekend. If you see that it's a clean load, your hostess will be forever grateful if you pitch in to empty it with her. Refilling it with dirty dishes from the sink will get you permanently on the "re-invite list." ;)

You wouldn't imagine how much firewood it takes to keep that large fireplace going! If you'd like to make Derek immensely happy, bringing in a fresh bagful of firewood from the front porch whenever you see it on the "low" side will also make you a Favorite Guest, likely to be re-invited again and again.

By now, you probably know how much Fabienne loves to cook for a crowd. However, if you feel like pitching in with a meal (breakfast or dinner) once during your stay, you are most welcome to do that. The Village Market is less than one mile away (left turn out of the driveway) and has most any basic thing you will need. (It's quaint— you'll like it.) For more elaborate meals, the next town over boasts two supermarkets, less than 15 minutes away if you turn right onto the main road out of the driveway. This is also a great place for outlet shopping, if you'd like to spend the afternoon doing that.

If you'd like to buy wine or other adult beverages, the gas station is a surprising option. This is located across from the Village Market, next to the mountain access road, less than two miles away (left turn out of the driveway). For more than basic wine choices, you may want to check out the wine stores in town.

If you need additional towels, they are located in the laundry room on the second floor. Upon your departure, feel free to put sheets and towels on top of the washer on the second floor (leaving the room looking neat is a plus). We'll take care of the rest.

We're so delighted that you've chosen to spend this time with us! Spending quality time with good friends and family is the single biggest reason we rent a house in Vermont for the season each year. Thanks so much for being in our lives.

Love, Derek and Fabienne

Notice the lighthearted, humorous tone and also the very specific instructions we use in the note. It's essentially a request on paper.

We've taped this sheet of paper above the counter every year, and I've been pleasantly surprised that without saying a word, our guests have pitched in above and beyond what I would have asked for. It really does work.

10. Stop right there

"No one can make you feel inferior without your consent."

—ELEANOR ROOSEVELT

In an ideal world, everyone you set standards and boundaries with will follow and uphold them. But sometimes, it takes several reminders for standards to sink in. Reinforcing a set boundary is as simple as saying one of the following, again in an even-keeled tone, without raising your voice or complaining.

- "Do you remember that request I made to you recently? I would like to remind you that it makes me uncomfortable when you do that. I'd really like your help in sticking with our agreement. It would mean a lot to me."

- "I'm not sure if you realize this, but what you just did and said is hurtful to me. We've spoken about this before. I'd like to request one more time that you not do that, please."

If it's said politely and with a calm demeanor, the offending person will take it much more seriously this time around and will feel caught in the act, which will usually elicit a favorable response.

At other times, however, you'll find yourself in a situation in which someone is doing something that is disrespectful. Perhaps a conversation you're having is becoming abusive, and there has been no standard set yet. This is when you must set a boundary immediately, even if it has never been communicated before.

I've done this many times in my life with friends, family members, my spouse, our children, and even clients. When someone repeatedly does something that is offensive or hurts my feelings, I calmly inform the person that this behavior is unacceptable and that if it continues, I will leave the conversation or the room. If it happens again, I will not continue seeing this person.

Again, the key is to enforce your boundary in an even-keeled tone, without yelling or shouting. I've made the mistake many times of yelling or shouting a "request," which didn't work. The person looked at me like I had gone mad or at least lost my cool—as if I were out of control. When you state your request and enforce a boundary, attaching a consequence to it, and do all of this without raising your voice, offenders stop in their tracks. Because you are calm and collected, they take you seriously.

Explain that the behavior is inappropriate. If you're just saying, "Stop doing that!" it will not be enough to communicate that this is not acceptable behavior around you. You must be very clear and specific. Part of being clear is that you must explain why this behavior is not acceptable. Is it disrespectful? Is it hurtful? Is it annoying? Is it dangerous? Otherwise, the person may just think you're being cranky and won't take you seriously.

Most often, the person will be taken aback by you making the request and will stop the offensive behavior.

But if it happens again, calmly remind the person about your boundary and let him or her know what the consequences of continuing the behavior will be. Again, this must be said without raising your voice, or you will be seen as unreasonable.

Stating consequences clearly communicates that you're serious. The consequence must be reasonable rather than an ultimatum. Some people react to ultimatums as a challenge or a threat. When people are backed into a corner, they often lash out, which is something you want to avoid.

Obviously, you must be prepared to follow through on the consequence if you want to be taken seriously, so never create a consequence you aren't willing to act on. Setting boundaries will have absolutely no effect if you don't consistently enforce the consequences you've set.

When you do this responsibly, little by little, all around your life, you will increase the quality of your life. People's behaviors will begin to change, their respect for you will grow, and you will no longer put up with behaviors that make you feel bad.

Conversely, you may experience some people falling away or spending less time with you. That's okay. If the only way they are happy spending time with you is when they can dishonor you, then you'll both be happier when they are somewhere else.

Have I fully mastered this in all areas of my life? With most people, yes, I calmly enforce my boundaries, without raising my voice. With my children, I am continually asking for their cooperation so we may work together on this. After all, I am a work in progress, as they are.

11. Zero obligations

"We have a duty not just to give to others, but to give to ourselves—and to see ourselves as worthy of receiving. We have a duty to honor others and to honor ourselves."

—PATRICIA SPADARO

You will encounter some people in life who are opportunists or bullies. They will want to use you or take advantage of you. It may be subtle, and they may do it with a smile, but these are people who will lead you off your path. They will do this without caring about your feelings or your preferences, or what the consequences will be for you. It will be advantageous for them, maybe even fun, to get you to do something they want that doesn't honor you or your choices.

Their tactics will feed off your need for approval or on your fear. Some will tell you that if you want to be included, then fulfilling their demands is what's required of you. Some will point out that everyone else you know is doing "it," and that you should too if you want to fit in. Some will threaten to leave you behind if you don't do what they want. Worse, they may threaten to hurt you. Without question, this is a form of bullying. It's manipulation, and people who do this are trying to take advantage of you.

I've experienced this innumerable times in my life, many more times than I could ever recall. As a woman, I feel that some people look at me as a target. Family members asked me to do things that I knew were fundamentally wrong. Boys in high school, college, and beyond pressured me to do things I didn't want to do.

Girlfriends bullied me to accept a certain type of behavior. Co-workers and bosses took advantage of me. Even in adulthood, there seems to be a silent consensus that says it's okay to take advantage of women and girls, and that their preferences don't matter.

This is not true. Your voice matters, and it's important that you honor your choices. Allowing someone to compromise you or dishonor you by making you do something you don't want to do is wrong. When you are asked to do something, check in with yourself before you say yes too quickly. Ask yourself if what is being requested of you will bring you joy. Is it meaningful to you? Will your budget allow it? Will you really have enough time? Will it affect your ability to care for yourself or your family? If the answer determines that the demand goes against your values, what you can (or want to) give, or what you want to do right now, then you have zero obligation to do it.

Recognize an opportunist—someone who thinks about his or her own needs before anyone else's. Their demands are a subtle form of bullying. Check in with yourself. "By asking me to do this, does this person also have my best interest in mind? Or just her own?" Consider your own needs. You don't always have to say yes. Does this person respect your time, money, energy, personal boundaries, and willingness to do this?

You are not a doormat. Do not give in to people who bully. Don't allow others to compromise you or take advantage of you. Others may want you to do something that, deep down inside, you don't want to do. They will give you every reason in the book why you should do it, or even force you to do it, making you question yourself and go against what you want.

Stick to doing things that honor you. Do not hesitate to say no. You can give an explanation if you want to, but know that you don't have to let them know why. You can simply say, "No, thanks, I'd rather not." This does not require further discussion. You're simply choosing not to.

A person of integrity will accept your decisions and will understand that no means no. Be kind, but be assertive. You are not obligated to give others what they want or do what they want, or to make personal sacrifices because they ask it of you.

Even if it's not the popular choice or if they threaten you, stick to your guns. The more you say no, the more you strengthen your self-esteem and self-love. You don't need their kind of negative approval in your life. When you have self-approval and self-love, no amount of outside approval is required. The more you say no, the easier it gets, and the more people respect you.

12. Best in class

"Perhaps we believe that we don't have the right to ask for more or feel like there isn't anything more than what we can see in front of us. But each of us does deserve the best that life has to offer."

—LOUISE HAY

In my childhood, there was always an emphasis on saving money and doing things in a bare-bones fashion. My father had grown up in France at a time when resources were extremely limited. As I was growing up, conversations focused on how much something cost, whether it was groceries, an article of clothing, or dinner out. Even now, I still get questions about how much my house cost and how many clients I have.

When I was able to get a bargain or pay less than retail, I was celebrated. Cheap was better and more honorable than expensive.

Generic items were seen as better than the name brand, because otherwise you'd be paying for the advertising and not the product.

Yes, we did splurge sometimes and ate well in restaurants, especially for our birthdays. And I respect the idea of not overpaying for the sake of overpaying, instead honoring the money that you do have.

At the same time, I created a meaning about myself that I didn't deserve to have the nicest, highest-quality things. I thought that I deserved second-class things, not the best in life. So when I got older, I bought cheap versions of clothing, shoes, and beauty products. I also spent time with cheap versions of people.

Certain moments stand out. One day I was debating whether to buy a beautiful cashmere scarf for $39 or the same style in chenille for $19. I held one in each hand, and while my heart was leading me toward the cashmere, my mind rationalized that I shouldn't spend so much on myself. So I bought the chenille one. I still have it, and every single time I wear it or look at it, my energy goes down, and I think, *You weren't good enough to deserve the beautiful cashmere one.* I know it's just a scarf, but it goes beyond the actual article of clothing to how I feel about myself.

For years, I'd say that I always wanted the best for my children. Then I would buy the generic pancake syrup for them, wanting to save those 20 cents. Not only did I not pay up for the real Vermont maple syrup that was available but I bought a product that was full of cheap corn syrup. I'm not sure my kids noticed any difference (at least until I started consistently buying the real maple syrup), but I certainly noticed it. Each time I took a bottle from the shelf and saw the supermarket brand, it chipped away at my self-worth and strengthened the belief that I wasn't worthy of the absolute best in class.

The more I've worked on my own growth and development, and the more I honor who I am and increase my self-worth, the more I've seen that I do deserve the very best quality in life. Nothing is too good for me. You deserve the same, too. In every aspect of your life—people, things, experiences—go for the very best quality you can afford. When you have choices, always choose the very best, even if you're not accustomed to it. It usually doesn't cost that much more. You deserve it, and the feeling you get really makes a difference.

Every time you make the lesser choice, you are telling yourself and the universe that you are not good enough to receive the very best the universe has to offer, that something's wrong with you, or that somehow you deserve substandard quality. That simply isn't the case.

If it's within your means, choose the higher-quality choice. Surround yourself with beautiful things. Even if you aren't making the kind of money you want to be making now, figure out something that will make you feel decadent. Maybe treat yourself to a bouquet of flowers from the supermarket each Monday morning. Or buy a beautiful crystal to hang in the window—the sun will provide the rainbows. Or buy a nicer soap than you typically get for yourself. When I was in my 20s, I was appalled to see that some premium liquid soaps sold for $20. I thought that was outrageous. Until the day I purchased one because it smelled so good. Each time I washed my hands, I felt abundant, beautiful, and that I deserved the very best in life. I know that it's just a little thing, but a high-quality liquid soap yields a lot of self-worth in every squirt.

The same is true of that candle you've always wanted but haven't purchased yet. Allow yourself to experience it. Each time you light it and smell its aroma, you transform how you feel about yourself. There are many, many opportunities for you to light it. You deserve it.

The idea is to create a more pleasing atmosphere to live in. Look around your living space and notice how it feels to you. Do you like what you see? Does it feel good to you? Does it raise your energy or decrease it?

Little by little, I recommend that you upgrade the quality of your entire life. Take out a sheet of paper and make a list of all the things you tolerate—instead of enjoy—about your environment, even if there's nothing you feel you can do about it now. Is there a rip in your bath towel? Are your shoes scuffed? Is your bedroom continually messy? What about your living room? Does it lack color? Look at your friendships. Whom or what do you tolerate? Write it down. Keep a long list of these things.

I made a long list of things I tolerate many years ago and have done it several times since. Each time I take the opportunity to look around at the things, people, and environments in my life and write down what drains my energy rather than supports it, I create an opportunity to improve my life.

Make it a goal to upgrade one thing each week. It can start small. Replace that ripped bath towel. Organize your desk. Just one effort per week to upgrade the quality of your life adds up to 52 improvements in a year.

Taking care of yourself in this way is an extension of loving yourself, and it feels amazing. Not only that but when you start surrounding yourself with beautiful things and upgrading your surroundings, then little by little you raise your healthy expectations of what you deserve in life. As a result, the universe sends you more things to be grateful about.

13. Top of the list

"Our first and last love is self-love."

—CHRISTIAN NESTELL BOVEE

If you love yourself first, everything in your life works. Too many times, we're taught to take care of everyone else before we take care of ourselves. The problem with that is there are way too many other things to take care of first. By the end of the day, there's no time or energy to take care of yourself. You go to the bottom of the priority list.

We spend a lot of time waiting to be loved and taking care of everybody else so that we can receive that love. When you take yourself off the priority list, you end up feeling empty and depleted. You no longer feel like you matter.

After being married for many years, having three kids, and running a very busy, very successful business, I looked around one day and saw that I'd lost myself. I had put my husband and my children at the top of the list, my business and my clients second, and my other family obligations next. Friends had fallen off the list and so had I.

I was not feeling very pretty. I was short-tempered, I was the most overweight I'd ever been, I was resentful that I had no time for myself, and I was stuffing down my feelings with food and wine. For years my weight climbed and my downtime got smaller and smaller. Yes, on the outside, I had everything I'd wanted, but I was missing a huge piece. Each obligation took me away from myself, to the point that I didn't know who I was anymore. I didn't feel as if I mattered, other than being of service to others in my life. I got resentful and began to care about myself even less. This went on for years.

What turned it around for me was to start taking care of myself and my looks. It may not be the perfect start for everyone, but throwing out loads of clothes that didn't fit right or make me feel good created space for other good things to come in. I began taking care of my appearance and felt better about myself on the inside.

Instead of whining that I wasn't getting the love or the downtime I needed, I started taking extra time in the morning to be by myself, to write in my journal and read. Little by little, I began making some healthy choices for breakfast. Lunch and dinner followed. Then I made nonnegotiable time for myself to just putter around and not have obligations for a couple of hours each week.

I own my own business. Most of the time, I don't see clients face-to-face, which means that I can dress ultra-casual for the office if I choose to. And I used to do this every day: yoga pants, T-shirt, fleece jacket, and clogs or sneakers. Often my hair hadn't been washed. I was completely uninspired.

One day, instead of feeling frumpy and going through the motions of my life, I planned what I would wear to work. The night before, I took the time to pick garments that flattered me. In the morning, I styled my hair, put on perfume, and added some jewelry, even a little makeup.

Who did I do this for? No one else but me. And as I kept doing this, I noticed that I started feeling lighter and happier. I loved myself more and took care of myself more. I ate better-quality foods in smaller portions to fit into my nicer clothes. I drank green smoothies in the morning instead of eating bread and butter. I lost weight and felt prettier. Again, I did all this just for myself.

My husband started to notice, so did co-workers, friends, and clients. Then, I watched my daughter start paying more attention to her own appearance. She now does something different to her hair every day. There's an even greater sense of self-confidence there. My older son combs gel into his hair before school, and it makes him feel proud to be able to do that for himself. My husband upgraded his wardrobe from an entirely ski-based clothing line to smart, tailored clothing that makes the most of his athletic build and good looks. My team members and employees slowly upgraded their looks, as well. And all this happened without me ever saying a word.

The key is that putting yourself back at the top of the list has a ripple effect, not just in the lives of others, but especially in your own life. For me, it started from the outside appearance and went inward. Through healthy food and making time for myself, I took better care of myself.

For you, it might be different. It might mean booking those horseback-riding lessons every weekend, painting, or running on the beach every morning. Perhaps it's learning a new language, taking a bubble bath after work, or going out to the movies every Wednesday night. It doesn't matter what you do to put yourself back on the priority list, as long as it starts now.

What I believe it comes down to is that we sometimes feel entitled to have other people in our lives fulfill the job of loving us. But loving yourself is your job. You can wait for someone else to fill you up with the love and care you want, but it will never be enough. When you expect love from an external source, and no one fulfills your void, then you will feel worse than before. To be able to be loved, you must love and respect yourself. This is the only dependable way to create lasting love in your life.

When you feel unloved and resentful on the inside, it's difficult to authentically give to others and love them back. When you love yourself first, you have much more to give because you're not trying to keep score. Making yourself a priority in your life is not a selfish thing. Doing this has changed my outlook on life, my relationships, how I speak to my husband and children, how I react in stressful situations, and my overall confidence and well-being.

14. Warts and all

"The worst loneliness is not to be comfortable with yourself."
—MARK TWAIN

It took me years, probably until I was in my late 30s, until I could seriously look in the mirror and say that

I liked myself, or that I thought I looked attractive. All those years of not fitting in and desperately trying to be part of an elusive tribe took a toll on my self-esteem. The majority of my life was spent in quiet self-revulsion and self-disapproval. Now I recognize it for what it was. I unfairly compared myself with others, and, as a result, I always felt like I didn't measure up.

I've discovered that constant comparison is a losing proposition because you don't see the whole picture. When you compare yourself with what others portray publicly, you don't ever get to see what they're really like behind the facade. You don't necessarily see their faults and flaws, only their best achievements. This results in you comparing apples with oranges, because you're judging your biggest shortcomings against other people's best appearances. You're measuring what you don't like about you against what you admire most in other people. This leads to an unfair assessment every time.

Understand that society and the media have projected a false ideal onto us. The measuring stick is held very high. There are so many false appearances going on in life in general, with people not telling you what it's really like or where they fall short, that it's a flawed competition.

If you try to measure yourself against a celebrity in a magazine photo, you're probably going to lose. Here's why.

- There's a whole team of makeup artists, stylists, and assistants dolling her up.

- The celebrity may have had plastic surgery that you don't know about.

- There is a great deal of airbrushing that goes on after the fact that results in the image you're staring at.

All of this creates a false ideal the celebrity herself could never measure up to in real life. Do you see the inequity here? As the Italian proverb goes, once the game is over, both the king and the pawn go back in the same box.

When you measure yourself against a false ideal, you can never be truly happy because there will always be an insatiable gap that cannot be filled. The more you try to fill it in vain, the more disappointed and depressed you will be, and the more it will affect your self-esteem. Instead, appreciate what you do like about yourself, and focus your attention there.

I have fallen in love with the French expression *jolie laide*. Literally, the term means "pretty and ugly at the same time." It doesn't actually refer to ugliness; rather, it focuses on the attractiveness of having unusual, flawed, or quirky good looks. A *jolie laide* woman has none of the typically pretty features of standard beauties, and yet she's extremely attractive.

What I've always loved about the term is that it refers to a woman who is magnetic and alluring, despite not being conventionally pretty. She's attractive because she has confidence, she knows how to carry herself, she likes herself as is, and she doesn't need outside acceptance to feel really good about herself. It's precisely this self-acceptance that makes her so irresistible. That inspires me.

You don't have to be "the whole package" to like yourself and feel confident in your own skin. The way that I began accepting myself was by saying, "I'm really good at a lot of things, and then there are some things I'm not good at. And I'm okay with that." It was the same with my looks. There are several things I'm pleased about regarding my looks and other things I'd change if I could. But since I can't, I'll just accept them for what they are.

Sure, I'm always looking to improve. But even if I don't, I'm now fundamentally pleased with myself as is.

Perhaps you don't compare yourself with others regarding looks. Instead, you measure yourself professionally against someone more successful than you are. They've got this and they've accomplished that. You see yourself as lower on the ladder of success, upset that it hasn't happened for you yet.

Realize that the person you're comparing yourself against may have many more years of experience than you do. You may not have seen the blood, sweat, and tears they've put in, the rejection, the persistence, and all that comes with success. What you see is only the result, the sheen and the gleam. But there is no such thing as an overnight success. There was probably a lot of sweat equity that went into the end result you see now. With the same sweat equity and determination, you too can see similar results one day. You must give yourself permission to be more realistic in your evaluations.

Begin to accept your flaws and like yourself as is. Part of loving who you are is being okay with (or at least beginning to accept) even the things you wish you could change. When you do this, you can slowly let go of the anxiety that comes with wishing things were different. You no longer need approval from the outside because you have it on the inside. You don't need security from others because you have security from within. You are no longer at the mercy of others for your happiness because you are happy enough with yourself.

Loving someone else unconditionally is accepting them just as they are, without making them feel bad for being less than perfect. The same applies to you. You are magnificent, you are beautiful, and you were created this way on purpose. There is only one you, and you are here for a purpose greater than you know.

15. Lalalala . . . I can't hear you!

"I had a boyfriend who told me I'd never succeed, never be nominated for a Grammy, never have a hit song, and that he hoped I'd fail. I said to him, 'Someday, when we're not together, you won't be able to order a cup of coffee at the fucking deli without hearing or seeing me.'"

—LADY GAGA

You'll always be a moving target for criticism and disapproval when you decide to play a bigger game and try to do things that others aren't willing to do, even when it's better for your life or for life as a whole. People don't like change, and they don't like it when you try to change. Whether you want to get healthier, grow personally, or do something that will make you more successful, when you reach for something bigger and better, it will invariably make some people uncomfortable.

Even those closest to you who would normally support you will try to talk you out of something that feels right for you. Why would someone who loves you try to slow down your progress? It's simply that your advancement can sometimes bring up other people's fears of change.

I'll never forget the day I decided to quit my corporate job in advertising sales to open up my own nutrition practice in 1999. It had taken me months to make the decision to leave, countless conversations, pro and con lists, and seeing clients on the side, as well as endless hours of preparation. The day had come to take the great leap of faith. I'd given my two weeks' notice at work. Instead of being scared, I was excited. A whole world of possibility and opportunity was now open in front of me, and I was giddy.

I called my closest friend and excitedly announced my news. There was silence on the line. Then, "Fabienne, I really think you're making a big mistake."

It was as if my balloon had been popped. We'd attended the same nutrition school at the same time, shared many what-if conversations about doing this professionally, and now that I was doing it, she met me with criticism. I was devastated.

I listened to her rationale about how I was making a foolish decision to walk away from a secure paycheck, that I was going to have a difficult time affording life in New York City being self-employed, and that I should rethink it.

I listened and listened, and I responded, "I appreciate your thoughts. I know they come from a good place. What I know for sure is that, right now, more than anything, I need to surround myself with people who believe in my future success. I need to surround myself with positivity because it's not going to be easy, but I will make it. So, I love you, and at the same time, I am asking you for some space while I make the leap. Will you give me that space?"

It probably took several months for us to speak again. By then I had a more secure footing, and our friendship was unaffected. When we reconvened and talked about what had happened, she told me that taking a financial risk as I'd done had brought up her fears around money. These fears had been passed down from her mother when my friend's father had (unsuccessfully) opened his own business. She was simply projecting her family's fear of taking risks onto my situation. It wasn't really that she disapproved; it was that her belief system was different from mine.

Sometimes when you reach for something bigger, it can bring up other people's feelings of inadequacy. I very clearly remember giving someone a tour of the new (much bigger) house we were purchasing a few years ago. It's a large home, and it was indeed a stretch financially from the mortgage we had been paying on our previous home. But once again, Derek and I had spent many months fact-finding, crunching numbers, and figuring out ways to afford it. Once we knew we could make it work, it was time to take the great leap of faith and put an offer on the house we wanted.

We expected friends who loved us to be excited for us. Instead, we were met with silence and quiet disapproval after giving them a tour of our soon-to-be home.

I don't believe that people consciously try to get in the way. I believe that they sometimes try to slow down your progress and talk you out of leaping to the next level. Perhaps it's because your growth reminds them that they're not making as much progress in their own lives as they wish they could. In the end, your growth reminds them of their own inadequacies. On the outside, they are trying to prevent you from making a mistake. But I believe on the inside, without even voicing it directly, they are probably thinking, *Who do you think you are, trying to be better than all of us?*

Let's face it. If you start doing something better for yourself, some people might resent you for it. At the same time, they may be afraid of you reaching for more and perhaps leaving them in the dust. They may be curious about their own growth, too, wondering if it would be possible for them to reach for new heights in whatever area of life they'd like to grow in.

Don't let others disparage you and knock down your ideas. Let the nay-saying slide off your shoulders. Do not pay attention. Love them, bless them, have compassion for them, but stay on task.

Now, obviously, I don't advocate making uninformed decisions. That's not responsible. The point is, if you know in your heart that you want to do something really good for yourself, you've done the due diligence to see that it will likely be a success, and you have the right resources in place, then go for it. Explain to anyone who tries to discourage you that you still love them and respect them, and you'll be there for them, but do not let anyone talk you out of it. Even if it's a bit scary and might make others uncomfortable, if your soul is asking for growth, then you should do it. If you don't grow, you're slowing dying.

16. It's okay to outgrow relationships

"It's no good trying to keep up old friendships.
It's painful for both sides. The fact is, one grows
out of people, and the only thing is to face it."

—W. SOMERSET MAUGHAM

Some relationships will stay with you forever, and some will be transitional and short-lived. When relationships don't work out, it's easy to blame yourself for needing to move on—or to blame someone else when he or she needs to move on. "And they lived happily ever after . . ." is an ideal that's ingrained in us, but it's often a fallacy.

Not all relationships need to live happily ever after. Some connections, positive or negative, are in your life to teach you a valuable lesson or to give you an experience you need for the bigger purpose of your life, whether you realize its importance in the moment or not.

There is a well-known poem that speaks to this relationship. While the author is unknown, the words have inspired people the world over:

> *People come into your life for a reason, a season or a*
> *lifetime.*
>
> *When you figure out which one it is,*
> *you will know what to do for each person.*
>
> *When someone is in your life for a reason,*
> *it is usually to meet a need you have expressed. They have*
> *come to assist you through a difficulty; to provide you*
> *with guidance and support;*

to aid you physically, emotionally or spiritually. They
may seem like a godsend, and they are.
They are there for the reason you need them to be.
Then, without any wrongdoing on your part or at an
inconvenient time,
this person will say or do something to bring the relation-
ship to an end.
Sometimes they die. Sometimes they walk away. Some-
times they act up and force you to take a stand. What we
must realize is that our need has been met,
our desire fulfilled; their work is done.
The prayer you sent up has been answered and now it is
time to move on.

Some people come into your life for a season, because your
turn has come to share, grow or learn.
They bring you an experience of peace or make you laugh.
They may teach you something you have never done.
They usually give you an unbelievable amount of joy.
Believe it. It is real. But only for a season.

Lifetime relationships teach you lifetime lessons; things
you must build upon in order to have a solid emotional
foundation.
Your job is to accept the lesson, love the person,
and put what you have learned to use in all other rela-
tionships and areas of your life.
It is said that love is blind but friendship is clairvoyant.

The lesson this writing teaches is essential: not every encounter or friendship will last, and that's okay. The relationship did what it was supposed to do.

Treasure what you had, whether you were the one to move on or the other person did it for you. Understand that, in the grand scheme of things, it's all perfect. You may not see it now, but some people aren't meant to be in your life forever. In fact, it's better that way. They have their own journey and you have yours.

When my husband, Derek, and I celebrated our tenth wedding anniversary, we watched our wedding on video. Instead of feeling as elated and grateful as I would have normally, I noticed that, out of the eight bridesmaids and eight groomsmen who shared that special day with us, we are no longer close friends with many of them, and we keep in touch with only a handful.

There was no blame or resentment. I take responsibility for this, but it did make me sad and a little depressed. Derek reminded me that we'd evolved a lot since then. We're not the same people we were, and naturally our friendships evolved, too. As we started to act more authentically like ourselves, we began to attract people who fit with who we truly are. Whether we chose to no longer spend time with someone or if the relationship just faded away, I realize that my life is better now because of it.

If someone chooses not to spend time with you, it will likely feel very hurtful. You will probably feel rejected. We've all experienced this at one point in our lives, and it's always painful at first. But with hindsight, you will realize that in the grand scheme of things, it was just time in your evolution to move on to different experiences.

If you're feeling bad about losing a friend—whether the choice was yours or theirs or simply came from the passage of time—the important thing is to think about the bigger picture. Try not to assign blame. Breathe. Journal your heart's feelings onto a page, many pages, over many, many days if necessary, and realize that this is what was supposed to happen. The sacred contract that you had and have now fulfilled was to learn something from each other. You are both no longer supposed to be in each other's lives. You've learned your collective lessons, and it's time to move on.

Let it be so, with no remorse, no anger, no blame . . . just be.

Chapter 2

Be the Most
Authentic You
That You Can Be

17. Who are you, really?

"God hath given you one face, and you make yourselves another."

—WILLIAM SHAKESPEARE

One of the things you hear most often in the personal-growth world is to "be yourself." In my opinion, that's not always easy. When I was young, I didn't have a lot of self-esteem. In fact, I believed that to be the best self that I could be, I had to be someone else. Because I felt that I wasn't good enough, I compensated by pretending to be something I didn't feel I was . . . smarter, more put together, more "something else" than I thought I was.

I put on a facade. I didn't lie exactly, but I put on a shiny, clean exterior, never letting anyone in, never letting people see what I truly felt or who I genuinely was. I never shared my feelings or my fears, and I made sure people thought I always had it together.

One day, after a phone call with some of my business colleagues, one of them called me back minutes later and said, "I respect you. You're very successful, and no one can question that. But there's this hard, cold exterior that we cannot get through. We want to know you, we want to like you for who you really are, but you're not showing that to us. I wish you'd just let us in."

At the time, I thought he was crazy. I didn't understand. I thought I was being open. But after hanging up the phone, I cried and cried. I knew deep inside that I wasn't being truthful in my interactions with others. I was hiding a part of myself in order to protect myself. I was afraid of what others would think about me if they really, truly got to know me and all my "stuff."

Yes, I had a lot of things in my life that I wasn't proud of. My mission at the time was to keep those things neatly hidden so that no one would ever see them. If people only saw the squeaky-clean, all-good side of me, maybe they'd like me.

I was afraid that if people found out who I really was, they wouldn't accept me. And so not only did I put on a fake exterior; I also pushed people away unknowingly. What I hadn't realized is that my fear of being discovered as a fraud, my worrying about what people would think of me if they really knew me, was alienating people, not bringing them toward me. In trying so hard to bring people into my life by showing only my good side,

I actually pushed them away. They could come just so close, because I only let them in a little bit.

After that phone call, I realized that I was doing myself a massive disservice by not being my authentic self with others. I was repelling the friendships I so craved. The only solution was to let others in, even if I risked them not liking the real me.

And so, little by little, in my work persona and in my personal life, I started sharing a teeny, tiny bit of what my real struggles have been and what they were at that time. And each time I did, I was met with compassion, love, and friendship. Very quickly and surprisingly, my life flourished and my relationships thrived (and some changed, admittedly). I will never go back to presenting someone other than my full self to people.

Surprisingly, the act of sharing more of my authentic self affected my business in a good way. The more vulnerable I was, the more prospective clients started coming out of the woodwork and acknowledging how refreshing it was to hear me be so truthful about my experiences, fears, and feelings. And they hired me. The more I shared the real me, the more clients I attracted, and the more successful I became. The more I shared openly about the little things in my life, the more I received confirmation that I wasn't the only one hiding behind a mask. And the more love and compassion I felt from others, the more I began to like myself. One of the greatest gifts is the freedom I now feel because I don't have to drag around that ball and chain of secrecy each and every day.

The more vulnerable you allow yourself to be, the more attractive you are. When you have your mask on, people energetically feel that you are not being authentic, and so they energetically don't trust you. Whether it's in business or in personal relationships, when you are not your authentic self or don't give fully of your real self, others do not give fully to you.

The ironic thing is, people see right through your mask, anyway. You can try to hide all the things you think you want to hide. You can do that for years, thinking no one suspects anything. But people will sense that something is fishy about you, that you're not fully being you. Even if they don't realize this on a conscious level, they certainly feel it on a subconscious level.

And so you repel the very people you want to be with, those who have a great sense of who they really are, those who have it together. You attract others who aren't authentic in their own lives. People who aren't genuine are not people you want to be with, because as they go against their true natures, they go in a direction that isn't good for them or you.

Here's how it works.

Energetically, you attract those who vibrate at the same level you vibrate. If you spend all your time and energy projecting yourself as something you are not, you naturally attract people who are projecting something they are not. This leads to destructive relationships.

The more authentic you are, the more clean energy you put forth. People feel that on an intuitive level. You attract others who are clean in their own energy. The more authentic you allow yourself to be, and the more cautiously vulnerable you are (in a good way), the more attractive you become to others. People will want to be with you, in relationships, in business—all around.

As Judy Garland once said, "Always be a first-rate version of yourself instead of a second-rate version of somebody else." Take the walls down. Let others in little by little. Let yourself be more transparent. That is your task. Be as authentic as you can be in every situation. You must come out from behind the mask and be vulnerable. In the end, the mask does not serve you; it actually harms you.

Am I suggesting you lay out all your dirty laundry for everyone to see? No. I took it one day at a time, one step at a time. Does it mean that you share too much all the time? No. There is a difference between personal things and private things. But between the two, there is a lot of room for you to be the most authentic you and be loved for it.

This might make others feel uncomfortable at first, especially if they've known you with your walls. But do it at your own pace. There is a huge sense of freedom in allowing others to see your true self.

18. Those who mind don't matter

*"Don't wish to be normal.
Wish to be yourself. To the hilt."*

—LOIS MCMASTER BUJOLD

I sometimes watch children's television shows with my kids, and I'm surprised that some of them portray such plastic emotions—impenetrable, implausible, and way too upbeat. It's as though the message is, "Only positive emotions and thoughts are acceptable." I see it perpetuated everywhere. I happen to be an incredibly positive and optimistic person, and yet it often seems to me that people are afraid to say what they think and feel.

I believe this is one reason we grow up thinking it's not okay to go against the norm, we're not supposed to speak up for ourselves, and confrontation is to be feared. We stuff our emotions and thoughts down, pretending we don't have any.

I dated a boy in my 20s who would often cut me off when I was talking in front of his friends. Whenever he did that, I felt as though he believed my words didn't matter, or I was less than him. One day, when he cut me off again in midsentence, I calmly looked at him and said, "I'm not finished." Then I continued my sentence. I wasn't rude about it in the least, but it was time to speak my truth.

I clearly remember his friends laughing at him. Some of them had their jaws open, shocked that I was taking a stand. I think that boy respected me just a little bit more from that day forward.

When it's time to think about what to have for dinner or what movie you'll watch with someone, too many people, especially women, will answer, "Whatever you want." They do not express their own wants, preferences, and opinions for fear of what others will think, say, and do.

It's important to let people know what you think and how you feel. In fact, it's the only way to live your life. If you don't feel that something is good, say so. If you feel disrespected, say so. If you don't feel right about a situation, say so. If you don't agree with something being said, say so.

That is the only way I know to respect and honor yourself and to live your most authentic life. In the end, those who care about you will respect you. Those whose feathers get ruffled were with you for the wrong reasons.

Obviously, this is not about being rude. It's about honoring how you want to be treated and sharing what you have to say. That said, if you have a track record of not speaking up, be prepared for consequences. You may throw some people off guard. It may turn them off because, up until now, you've misrepresented yourself. Through this misrepresentation, you may have attracted people who were with you only because you didn't rock the boat—because you were a people pleaser.

Yes, in being authentic with your thoughts and emotions, you might ruffle feathers. But I'll tell you this: I would much prefer to be alone and fully self-expressed than to be with others who shut me down and make me feel as if my opinions don't matter.

I believe in being authentic in my work, too. Although it took me many years to get up the courage to add the words *high-achieving* and *go-getter* to my website and marketing materials regarding the clients I would like to have, I'm grateful I did. As a high-achieving go-getter myself, I work best with other high-achieving go-getters who know what they want and are super-ready to get going. By stating my truth, I was able to attract the clients I'm best suited to work with. And I set boundaries, letting people know that these are the types of people I want to work with. Stating this up front allows me to cherry-pick my clients, and to gently turn away people who aren't suited for my programs and won't get the results they would have signed up for. (It wouldn't be fair to them otherwise.)

Another bit of information that I included in my marketing materials is the type of person I won't work with: the chronic skeptic and whiner, someone who consistently complains, makes excuses for not getting assignments done, or challenges every aspect of the program. If you are one of these people, I gently and respectfully ask that you not call. I hope you understand why. We probably will not work well together, and I wouldn't want you to waste your time or money. Is that fair?

Some might think that's a negative statement to add to one's marketing materials, but I've found that expressing myself in this way before speaking with a prospect acts as a filter for just the right types of clients for me. It may offend some people (the chronic skeptics, whiners, and complainers), and that's okay; they've now stopped calling.

Please know that I don't mean to sound callous. That's not my personality. Rather, I realized that I was doing others a disservice and wasting their time by not stating who I work well with and who I am not the right match for. Now I only get calls from people who believe the same things I do. And that feels good for me.

A surprising side effect I never anticipated is that ideal clients, those I love working with, often tell me that the moment they read those words was the exact moment they knew in their hearts they wanted to work with me. They said a silent, "You go, girl!" when they read it. They respected me on the spot.

I'd like to give you permission to speak your truth and be true to yourself, no matter what the reaction may be. Tell people how you feel and express yourself fully. Speak up to say what you think. That is true freedom.

Caveat: Some people use the idea of being "fully self-expressed" as an excuse for being hurtful, especially online. I call this "Keyboard Confidence" and it's just plain rude. If you wouldn't say it to a person's face, then don't say it online.

19. I lean this way

*"The person born with a talent they are meant to use
will find their greatest happiness in using it."*

—JOHANN WOLFGANG VON GOETHE

Embrace your natural inclinations. There are things you do that no one else does as well as you do. Your unique brilliance activities are those that you could do all day long and get an immense sense of joy from. You keep getting better and better at these activities, and people recognize you for them. You tend to lose track of time when you do them. In fact, you love doing these activities so much that you catch yourself doing them for free.

Pay attention to these activities. This is where you are uniquely brilliant (even if you take it for granted), and it's one of the things that makes you magnificent.

Understand that you are naturally wired to do certain things very, very well. You were born with this, you will have it forever, and it is one of the keys to your lasting happiness. For some, it's speaking onstage; for others, it's writing. Perhaps it's painting, skiing, cooking, teaching, building, or creating sacred spaces.

The more you can recognize the unique talents that were given to you, single them out, and spend more of your time doing them, the happier and more successful you will be.

We discount this because we are taught to be well-rounded, that we should get better at the things we're not good at. Nothing could be more false. If you spend your life trying to become good at something you'll never really be good at, this will affect your self-esteem. It will make you feel like you are simply not good enough and will eventually chip away at your confidence.

On the other hand, if you spend the same amount of time getting better and better at the things you are naturally gifted at, you will get infinitely better at these. You will feel a great sense of accomplishment and joy, and experience a huge amount of confidence.

I'll give you an example. I've never been really good at numbers, especially bookkeeping. When I opened my first business, the last thing I wanted to do was tally up my accounts, spend time looking at my budget, and, most of all, file my taxes. In all transparency, I was late on my taxes for many years in a row during the first few years of my business. Nothing made me unhappier than to work on the numbers.

Believe me, I tried many times. I would take a full Saturday, lock myself to my computer, and after a whole day of effort, I would be absolutely, totally miserable. I got the job done, but not very well. And I felt depleted, frustrated, and resentful knowing that I'd wasted a Saturday doing this.

But what did make me happy was marketing my business, closing the sale with an ideal new client, or creating a new product that would make a difference in people's lives. I can do that all day long, and I am very good at it. In fact, in just a few hours, I can create a new program that will ultimately bring in big sums of money. That's much more fun for me than the minutia of working on tax paperwork and tracking expenses.

When I first started dating my now-husband, he was shocked to find out about the state of my finances. One of our first arguments was about this. He couldn't understand why I didn't have my bookkeeping in order. To him, math and finances come naturally. He's always been good at it, and it's a breeze for him to make sense of it all. I remember saying to him, "If I had spent the same amount of time doing something I'm naturally good at that I spent on my bookkeeping, I could have made several thousand dollars."

This is when we both agreed that it was time for a bookkeeper to come in and take this work out of my hands—someone who happened to love numbers and could work on my finances for me, at a fraction of the monetary and psychic cost. This was one of the best investments I ever made in myself. The same was true when I hired a housekeeper. The time that I used to spend on accounts and cleaning, I now use to get better at the things I'm already naturally good at.

Take a look at your natural inclinations. What are the things that you do very well, that people recognize you for, and that you would do all day long for free and still have energy to spare? These are your unique brilliance activities.

Then look at the things that you do that you're not very good at, either at work or at home. What activities drain you, make you feel resentful, and inspire the desire to delegate them or simply stop doing them?

The more hours you spend doing the things you are naturally inclined to be good at, the happier and more successful you will be.

Chapter 3

Do the Right Thing

20. Integrity changes your life

"Have the courage to face the truth. Do the right thing because it is right. These are the magic keys to living your life with integrity."

—W. CLEMENT STONE

Some of the unhappiest moments of my life and the source of experiencing lower and lower self-esteem were the result of me not doing the right thing in particular situations. I knew what was right a lot of the time, and I chose to ignore it and do its opposite. The list would take up its own book, but here are just a few of the things that come to mind:

- Not returning a pair of shoes I borrowed from a friend in college

- Stealing makeup from the grocery store when I was in middle school
- Copying a friend's essay verbatim and handing it in as my own to the same teacher she had had the previous year
- Saying to my mother that I was somewhere I wasn't
- Lying repeatedly to my friends in grade school
- Getting caught by a potential employer for lying on my résumé
- Telling my dad I'd sent him letters when I hadn't
- Not refunding a client in full during my early years in business
- Leaving the futon in front of my apartment when I moved out

There are countless ways I didn't do the right thing when presented with an opportunity to do so. These made me feel like the lowest of the low, a fundamentally bad person. The shame and regret were overwhelming.

These were things that I had to hide from others so they wouldn't see all that was wrong with me. All those times that I chose the path of doing the wrong thing, even though I knew better, contributed to my spiraling loss of self-esteem and feelings of unworthiness.

Until a few years ago, when I started noticing that when I did the right thing, even if I was the only one who knew it, I liked myself in that moment. The more

I acted with integrity in everything I did, the more my life changed for the better. I became happier. My self-esteem grew. I was more confident. I was infinitely nicer to myself.

I've come to realize that being a person of integrity is simply being someone who chooses to do the right thing, even when no one's watching—especially when no one's watching. That could mean little things, such as always washing your hands after going to the bathroom, even when you don't feel like it; not peeing on the toilet seat in a public restroom or at least cleaning it up; not redipping a spoon into the sauce when you're cooking for others (even when they'd never know it); always washing your hands before cooking; telling the truth; letting the cashier know that she forgot to charge you for a particular item; or paying a friend back on time (if not early and with interest). If you misplace something that you borrowed, then replace it. Put clothes back on the hanger in the department store dressing room. Empty the dishwasher when you are a guest in someone's home.

For some people (and this was me many years ago), morality is doing what you want and not getting caught. The problem with that is you slowly chip away at your self-esteem each time you do something you know isn't right. It puts a chasm between a person of integrity and the person you are being in that moment.

My solution for choosing integrity in each moment is to act as if a video camera is always on me and my life is being broadcast on television. Imagine living your life as if people were able to see everything you are doing and saying. Imagine what would change about your behaviors. Looking at your actions this way helps you trust yourself. It gives you a moral compass, a code of rules that's easy to follow.

The idea is to strive for integrity, always. Will you be perfect in doing this 100 percent of the time? Probably not. We all slip sometimes. But I'll tell you that, with practice, you can get really good at this living with integrity thing, because it feels so good. When you live this way, an incredible feeling washes over you, a feeling that you are indeed a good person, that you've done the right thing. This gives you massive amounts of self-love and confidence. In my experience, it also helps you erase the shame and the feelings of unworthiness from times when you didn't act with integrity.

A person with integrity is someone who does the job right and does not take shortcuts or cheat to get the end result. It means that you are honest, reliable, and trustworthy. It helps others trust you, especially if you haven't necessarily lived with integrity in the past. If you've previously lied, cheated, and stolen, then those around you probably don't trust you very much. And they're probably not going to trust you any time soon unless you show them a different way of living your life.

The more you live your life with integrity, doing the right thing at every opportunity, the more these same people will notice and, over time, have trust in you again. Consistency is key.

To become a person of greater integrity, would you change the way you do certain things now? Would you act differently? Would you speak differently? What would change?

21. Are they in the room?

"Who gossips to you, will gossip of you."

—TURKISH PROVERB

Have you ever heard others talking about you in a negative way when they didn't know you could hear them? How did you feel? Betrayed, angry, hurt? I remember when I was 11 or 12 years old and at a slumber party. As I was trying to fall asleep, I heard two other girls say things about me that they probably didn't want me to hear. It crushed me and made me feel very isolated. I let it affect my self-esteem for more than 20 years.

Nothing good ever comes from talking badly about others, whether they can hear you or not.

I created a meaning about myself based on what I overheard, and that meaning was that I was unlovable and didn't fit in. This affected my life every day and in every way, dictating my actions and choices.

The solution that works for me? Only speak about others if they are in the room with you and participating in the conversation, or as if they were. Would your choice of words be different in that situation? Would you say that if they were there, listening to you?

It's amazing how something that may seem so insignificant can create damage for someone on a long-term basis. You wouldn't want someone to talk about you in a negative way, so don't talk about others like this.

I realize how difficult this can be when others begin the conversation. I continually get sucked in to this kind of conversation. When I catch myself participating, the thing that I've discovered works best is to say, "You know, I really believe in only talking about someone as if they were in the room. Right now, I wouldn't feel comfortable having her hear this. So I think we should talk about something else. I know I wouldn't want someone talking about me this way." It usually makes everyone involved realize they wouldn't want others to talk about them in that way, either, and the conversation quickly moves to another subject.

When you are involved in a conversation with someone who gossips, the likelihood is that they will gossip about you when you aren't there. By not participating, you are making a statement that this is not acceptable for you and you don't approve of it.

22. Own up to the pretense

"Sometimes letting things go is an act of far greater power than defending or hanging on."

—ECKHART TOLLE

Have you ever caught yourself in the middle of an argument and realized the other person was right and you were wrong—but you kept defending your point of view? There comes a point when both you and the other person realize that you are now defending your side for the sake of defending it, not because your position is valid.

It is a critical point in many relationships, when honor, respect, and trust collide with integrity and truth.

It may not seem like a big deal at the time, but what you do in that moment greatly determines your character. I urge you, when the time is right, to apologize midargument. Whether it's as small as arguing over a game of *Monopoly* or something deeper or more meaningful, the right thing to do is to give up on that argument when you know the other person is right, and let that person know he or she is right.

The argument will stop right there, as there is no longer a reason to disagree, and you will instantly gain respect from your adversary. The process of letting go of a false pretense makes you feel better as a person. It builds your self-respect and self-love, which then affect your confidence, which in turn touches every aspect of your life.

Try this tactic of owning up to your imperfections in the midst of an argument. Instead of saving face, fess up to your part in it. Take personal responsibility and act with integrity. Apologize for your part in the argument and you will defuse things immediately. This disarms the person you were arguing with and brings everything back to normal within minutes.

I have found this to be very useful in my marriage, and especially with my children. If you can own up to your kids for making a mistake or not being right, they will have much more respect for you in the long run. They will also pay attention when you have conviction about something in future conversations. It likewise works with clients and friends.

It's about being authentic in all your dealings and having integrity in your life. When you do, people trust you, and that is a very worthwhile thing.

23. Everyone has pain

"When I am able to resist the temptation to judge others, I can see them as teachers of forgiveness in my life, reminding me that I can have peace of mind only when I forgive rather than judge."

— GERALD JAMPOLSKY

It's easy to talk about other people and judge them for their actions, their appearance, or what they've said. I remember what a former neighbor of mine said one night during a barbecue in my backyard. Several people were talking about a situation, which led to talking about a person, and then to judging that person pretty harshly. At first, I got caught up in it and found myself judging, too, until I stopped myself. I shared my feelings about only talking about a person as if they were in the room, and then I added, "Let's not judge her."

The response from my neighbor was, "Why not? It's fun to judge!"

I was so stunned by that statement that I didn't know what else to say. Maybe I judged her quietly in that moment. More important, I got an insight into what makes people tick. I realized that when you judge someone or something, you get a quick high from it, a sense of superiority that feels elevating. I wondered if judging others somehow makes us feel better about ourselves for a brief moment.

Sure, it's easy to judge. When someone's not the same as you, it's an easy reflex to make them wrong, to put yourself in a superior position, especially when you feel inferior inside. I remember an incident in high school when my best friend got onto the cheerleading squad and

I didn't. She was now running in a fast-moving crowd of popular girls and didn't have much time for me anymore. I felt small, insignificant, useless, and unpretty, especially when I compared myself with all those tanned, long-legged, high-stepping girls who I perceived had taken my friend away.

So I started to judge them, at first quietly, and then to others. I took them down whenever I could. I made myself out to be superior to them, when inside all I felt was inferior. It was a self-preservation method, and it felt good while I was doing it. But it made me feel even worse about myself afterward. I thought, *If I am so harshly judging these girls whom I don't know, am I going to be judged similarly in the future by others who don't know me? How would that feel?*

Sometimes we judge instinctively, without realizing we do it or the harm that it causes. One of the greatest regrets I have is again something I said in high school. I remember walking to class with a male friend. We were chitchatting about the upcoming prom.

When he told me whom he'd asked (and I cringe telling you this), I responded, "Really? You could do so much better than her!"

The look of horror, anger, and betrayal on his face has never left me. I lost that friend on the spot. I regret this because I hadn't meant what I said. I had never really known the girl. But I felt compelled to judge and make myself feel superior. I felt ugly doing it, and still today I wish I could take it back and apologize to her in person.

Often, people feel justified in judging because "clearly" there's a lot to judge. But do we really know what's happening behind the scenes, what someone has gone through in life, or what that person is going through right now? You know the saying, "Don't judge a man until you've walked a mile in his shoes."

Everyone experiences pain. Most times, we don't show our pain to others. And yet we act from that pain. That's what happened to me.

I was the target of a lot of judgment, bullying, and criticism when I was younger. I was different, lost, and unguided. I did and said things that were completely inappropriate. I now know that it was because I was broken inside. I was desperate to find a place where I belonged, to know who I was, and to find a day when I could love myself—heck, even just like myself. But no one knew this on the outside. They were judging me based only on my outside.

Not too long ago, I was at a dinner party hosted by good friends. Another couple joined us. They told a story of watching an obese woman in a diner who was staring out into space. With one hand she was eating French fries, and with the other smoking a cigarette. She appeared dazed. They related that at one point, she put the cigarette in her mouth as if it were a French fry and started to chew it. In recounting this story, they judged her harshly for being obese, for dazing out, for eating French fries, for smoking to begin with, and then for eating her cigarette.

I immediately thought that there must have been a reason this woman was so numbed out with food and cigarettes. She was trying to stuff down an internal wound, a deep-seated pain. Who's to say she wasn't the victim of a horrible experience or set of circumstances? If you really played out the scenario, there are millions of things you can imagine having happened to that woman in the diner.

If we could have compassion for her and her pain, if we could begin to see her as a wounded soul in need of love and compassion, then perhaps we could forgive her that pain and, most important, her coping mechanism. Don't we all have a coping mechanism?

Does having compassion mean we champion the coping mechanism of choice? No. But understand that all pain is the same at its core, and we all have experienced it in differing degrees. We all carry around some pain. When we judge others, we're really judging that same aspect of ourselves. When I said to my friend, "Really? You could do so much better than her!" I was really speaking to myself about my own flawed relationship. I could have been doing better but had chosen to stay in an abusive relationship. I just didn't realize a mirror was being held up for me at the time.

I've caught myself talking in a disparaging way about another in the recent past because I felt entitled to, especially after "what she did to me." I was set on getting revenge. Talking about her made me feel that I was quietly getting back at her in a way that she couldn't defend against. (Yes, I know that's passive-aggressive. I recognize it now.) I believed at the time that she deserved it. Yet this is another form of abuse. And there's no excuse for it.

I've since made a commitment to avoid talking disparagingly about others. It's not always easy, especially when someone has trespassed against me. But it's an act of violence any way you look at it. Would I say those things if that person were standing there? No way. And when you judge someone else, you judge yourself at the same time and will do so for years to come.

Chapter 4

Take Personal Responsibility

24. Are you responsible for this?

*"Everything that exists in your life exists because of you,
because of your behavior, words, and actions."*

—BRIAN TRACY

There was a time in my life when everything seemed
to go wrong. I was in abusive relationships, I wasn't eating properly, I was having trouble at work, I was consistently on the verge of being evicted from my apartment
because I was not paying my bills on time (in fact, I was
simply not opening the bills), I wasn't making enough
in my job, my American Express card was shut down
because I couldn't pay the $4,000 balance from the cu-
linary school I enrolled in (which I knew I couldn't afford), and I was unhappy. I kept looking around, trying

to find the reason for all this chaos, and blaming my circumstances for the fact that I didn't have the life I wanted.

But then one day it dawned on me that the common denominator in all the things that were going on was me. Everything I touched turned bad. I was the one who was in control of everything that wasn't going well.

Little by little, I started to own up to things. One step at time, I took personal responsibility for every aspect of my life. If I wanted to reduce my $15,000 credit card debt, I needed to open the bills and pay them on time. If I wanted to be paid more, I needed to do a better job—then ask for a raise. If I wanted to have better relationships, then I needed to get out of the crummy one I was in. And so on and so forth.

I've come to realize that everything I am and everything I have is completely up to me. Everything that exists in my life exists because of my words, my actions, and my choices. The same is true for you.

Because you have free will and freedom of choice, because you choose each and every action you take in your life, you are completely responsible for all of your success and failure, your happiness and unhappiness. You have personal responsibility for your past, present, and future.

This is a difficult concept to grasp for some because it means that you must point the finger toward yourself, as opposed to outside of yourself. But the concept of accepting personal responsibility is what separates an adult from a child, a successful person from one who is a failure. It's the rite of passage for maturity.

While there are definitely outside factors that play a part, you can choose how to deal with them. You can let them stop you or you can figure out how to get beyond them. You create your life. No one else does.

Think about it in terms of weight management. If I'm not willing to change my eating behaviors by reducing my intake of foods that are not good for me and increasing my intake of foods that are healthy, then I can't possibly complain about how fat I look.

If I'm not willing to add more movement in my life, then I can't possibly whine that my weight isn't what I want it to be. It's my personal responsibility what I put in my mouth and how much moving I do. I understand that. In fact, there's a saying in my house: "You can't complain about something you're not willing to change."

Only you think your thoughts. Only you decide what you'll read and listen to. Only you choose whom you'll associate with and the conversations you'll engage in. Therefore, you are totally responsible for all the consequences of all those behaviors. The logic is unavoidable.

You create your life with every action you take and with every action you don't take. Every decision, every fork in the road you encounter gives you an opportunity to create your life and shape it a certain way. With every opportunity life presents to you, you have an opportunity to change course. In every moment, you can begin making different choices.

So if you aren't living the life you want, it isn't a product of your circumstances, but a product of your actions. The key to making your life different is in your hands. You can change your life, starting today, by changing your thoughts, your actions, what you focus on, and what your habits are. When you do, you change your life.

If you want things to be different, look around for others who are experiencing what you want to experience or who have what you want to have. Then look at what they're doing differently from what you're doing. Do those exact things, and stop doing the things that don't directly get you closer to your goal.

Your new mantra can be, "I am responsible." The more you say this, the more you'll see every single aspect of your life improve.

25. Point that finger elsewhere

*"When it looks like everyone is against you,
look inside for the truth."*

—SUMNER DAVENPORT

Blame is the opposite of taking personal responsibility. Blaming others for what you don't like about your life gives you an excuse for not doing the work of creating the life you want. It takes the power right out of your hands. By blaming others, you are saying that an outside person or situation has complete control of you. You are saying that your life is totally dependent on the action of others. But this isn't true. If you want change, then you must change. This is why you must take personal responsibility for your every action. Every result is yours to own and only yours.

When it comes to how we look at living our lives, I believe that there are two diametrically opposed ways that people think. There are those who believe that they were born into a certain way of life and were meant to live that life, without the ability or control to change it much. The cards have been dealt, and they feel they must play that hand, good or bad.

Then there are people who believe that they can indeed create their situations, create their income, and create their lives. They believe they shape everything they're experiencing. They keep asking the dealer for another set of cards until they have a better hand to play and can win at this game of life.

Most people hang out somewhere between these two extremes. What really matters and what changes lives is the concept of personal responsibility. Whether you believe that you can manufacture almost every single aspect of your life or not, the likelihood is that you understand that you are responsible for at least some aspect of what you've created for yourself. What I've noticed from years of working directly with entrepreneurs who are looking to make more money in their businesses is that, in the rare event that things don't work quickly enough, the blame comes out. People are quick to blame the process, another person, their coach, the economy, the weather, their bank balance, or anything else to deflect their own responsibility in the matter. People will do anything but take responsibility for and ownership of what's been created, especially when they haven't done the work required for results.

Those people who are truly successful in their lives take full responsibility for everything, and I mean everything. Failures in their lives are simply errors in judgment and decision making. Those who blame are acting like victims and will never reach their full potential.

Take for example the people who set big goals for themselves. If that goal seems a bit out of reach, notice that many people have an excuse in their back pockets, just in case the goal isn't reached. As soon as things get hard, those in avoidance and denial pull out their "blame card" to let themselves off the hook. But that won't get them anywhere in the long run. I've experienced it, and it gets you nothing except more of the same.

In the end, unless you're willing to keep living exactly the same scenario that you're living now, the first thing you must do is take a cold, hard look at where you put the blame for what you don't have, and how often you do so. Your life will begin to change, and you'll be that much closer to attracting what you do want.

26. Clean up that mess

"It is the highest form of self-respect to admit our errors and mistakes and make amends for them. To make a mistake is only an error in judgment, but to adhere to it when it is discovered shows infirmity of character."

—DALE E. TURNER

Once you realize how important it is to stop blaming, to take personal responsibility for your life, and to stop lying, the next step is to own up to your mistakes.

We all make mistakes. It's part of life. Even though you may think you're the only one who makes as many mistakes as you do, that simply isn't true. Everyone does. You just don't see others' mistakes because many happen behind closed doors.

I believe that behind every slick exterior reside a lot of secrets and mistakes. That's why I'm being more transparent in my own life than ever before.

There is no reason to feel ashamed of the mistakes you make. The universe doesn't judge you for them and neither should you, however difficult it is for you to avoid doing that.

With all these things you regret stashed away in your consciousness, it's difficult to feel good about yourself. That's what happened to me. The longer the list of shameful moments, the more you quietly beat yourself up. In turn, this affects your self-confidence and self-esteem, which affect all other areas of your life.

You must take personal responsibility for your actions, especially those you aren't proud of. This is the only way to be freed from the guilt and shame that lead to feelings of inadequacy.

Own up to your errors in judgment to yourself first, knowing that when you made these errors, you may not have been thinking. You may have chosen to ignore your intuition. You may not have had the knowledge or experience you have now that would have prevented you from taking that action.

Make a list of all the mistakes you've made and all the things you regret doing or saying. No one ever needs to see this list. It's for you and only you. See it as a safe space to be fully honest about everything you've said or done. Write down everything you can think of. Keep adding to the list. This is not to make you feel worse. It's an exercise in getting it out of your head and onto a sheet of paper, someplace outside of yourself.

Then do what you can to clean up the mess. Fix what you can. Tell people you're sorry and mean it.

Let me share with you an example from a while ago. When I was single and living in New York, I went to a New Year's Eve party at a friend's apartment on Park

Avenue. It was a sumptuous place and a great party. We were having a wonderful time. After too many margaritas, I was in the kitchen and somehow, right behind me, the glass door of the oven shattered into thousands of pieces.

I didn't see what happened, didn't take personal responsibility for it, and told the host, my friend, that I didn't know what had happened.

But deep down inside, I knew. I just knew that I must have had something to do with it, even though my mind wasn't clear enough to remember exactly what happened. And I was scared to be responsible for the cost of replacing such an expensive oven when I didn't have much money. So I chose the avoidance and denial route, which filled me with remorse, even though I didn't see an alternative at the time.

This guilt sat with me for years and years. Every time I thought about it, a sinking feeling would come over me and make me feel like I was a worthless person. I couldn't shake it.

Years later, I ran into the same friend, the host of the party, at an event, and I took him to the side. I was nervous, but I got up the courage and apologized sincerely and from my heart. I told him that I should have taken responsibility for my actions years before, and that I should have paid for the expense of the oven back then. I was relieved when he seemed really appreciative of my apology, even though it had come so many years later.

I also offered to give him a check for several hundred dollars to pay for the expense of the replacement oven door. He suggested instead that I write a check to a foundation we both supported. Writing that $400 check was one of the best feelings ever. It was my way of cleaning up my mess and making it better, even years later. It helped me heal that part of myself that was judgmental about my actions and, most especially, my avoidance and denial.

Over time, I've fixed as many things on my list as I could. For some, I poured my feelings onto a piece of paper or into a journal, giving voice to the part of me that felt sorry. Each time, I raised my self-esteem and felt so much better.

What about you? What's on your list? What will you do to apologize and clean up your messes?

Doing so will make you feel better, and people will respect you more—but, more important, you'll respect yourself more.

27. The company you keep

"You are the average of the five
people you spend the most time with."

—JIM ROHN

Part of taking personal responsibility for creating a rich, full, abundant life you love includes taking into consideration the people with whom you spend the most time. The Law of Association states that who you spend your time with, and whom you listen to and take advice from, dictates your life. Who you associate with shapes who you are. Who you spend time with is who you quickly become.

That being said, be very careful about the company you keep.

I believe that environment is everything. For example, if you're looking to get healthier and eat more vegetables, fruits, and whole grains, it is infinitely easier to do this when your fridge is filled with beautiful vegetables than when your cabinets are filled with sugary, processed foods. It is also easier to reach your health goals when you spend time with people who are already healthy, rather than those who regularly make choices that aren't aligned with the results you seek.

If you are looking to become a better skier, then skiing with people who are slightly more advanced than you are or taking regular lessons with an expert ski instructor will give you a better chance to improve your skills, than spending more time with those who struggle to get down the bunny hill.

If you'd like to make more money in your career, attempt to spend more time with people who are advancing, those who are doing well and making progress, rather than those who struggle. Otherwise, it's easy to get caught up in other people's negativity, cynicism, small thinking, fear, and doubt. You can accelerate your level of abundance by surrounding yourself with people who are already living big and those happily headed there.

Study those who are already living a life you want. Learn everything you can from them. Study their lives, read their books or biographies, spend time with them, attend their seminars, and mentor with them if you can. You can even model their behavior if it's in alignment with who you want to be and it's in your highest good and the highest good of all.

There was a time in my career when I decided I wanted to multiply my business quickly. I had done lots of personal growth and spiritual development work to eliminate some of my limiting beliefs and fears about growing my business and I was ready to start playing bigger. Instead of looking sideways at what other colleagues of mine were doing to market their businesses, what they were charging, and with whom they were associating, I decided to look up the ladder.

What I mean by "looking up" is that instead of looking for someone who was just a few steps ahead of me, I searched my industry and similar industries for someone whose business was producing revenues that were at least ten times what mine were. When I located someone and found out this person could mentor me for a fee, I decided to invest in myself and signed up for two years of coaching.

My results and income in those two years skyrocketed. The learning curve of growing my business became so much more manageable. I learned about best practices in business, but I also learned about how already successful people think and act. I studied how they lived and modeled their behaviors.

Once I'd reached my initial goal and felt ready to move on and multiply to another level, I once again looked up the ladder for someone who was achieving ten times the revenues I was now achieving. I signed up to be mentored by that person's company, too, learning best practices and spending time with the other students who were happily looking to grow their own businesses. And I dramatically increased my results once again. Now whenever I'm ready to make a change in my life (or my business), I look up the ladder and ask myself, "Who's achieving what I'm looking to achieve, and how can I model what they're doing or learn from them directly?" This has proven to be a very successful strategy for me, and it is one that I now provide to my own students.

Now it's your turn. Ask yourself, "Right now, who is where I wish to be? Who is living a life that I'd like to live? Who do I want to be when I grow up?" Name at least one person who fits this category. Then make a plan to immerse yourself in learning everything you can from them. I've learned that this is the shortcut to bypassing an otherwise long learning curve. Over a short period of time, this new way of thinking and viewing life becomes your new normal.

The Law of Association also states that what you create in life is directly proportionate to the expectations of your peer group. That being said, how are the people you spend the majority of your time with now affecting your life, either positively or negatively? If you were to spend *less* time with someone, who would it be? Who would you spend *more* time with?

I'm not suggesting you ditch your family and current friends. You may simply want to add some new people to listen to and spend time with:

- People who think positively about their future, and yours

- People who are positive

- People with an abundance mind-set

- People with a high level of emotional intelligence (rather than those who thrive on drama)

- People with the same core values you have

- People who take personal responsibility for their lives (rather than those who

blame, criticize others, or continually make excuses)

- People who champion you when you attempt a big goal, who celebrate you when you accomplish something big, and who provide a soft place to land when things aren't going your way

- People who are already where you want to be or happily getting there

Find these people and join their tribe if you can. If this is not possible, then create your own tribe according to the parameters I've listed above. That's when you achieve so much more than you would on your own.

Chapter 5

Forgive Yourself

28. A flashlight in dark corners

"Shame is felt as an inner torment, a sickness of the soul. . . .
The humiliated one . . . feels himself naked, defeated,
alienated, lacking in dignity or worth."

—SILVAN TOMKINS

Beyond simple mistakes and acts of avoidance and denial, there are also deeper things that we regret and feel shameful about. Shame is one of the things that will take you down and keep you down. It's an insidious, ugly feeling.

The more shame you feel about yourself and your life, the less you feel good about yourself, the less you like yourself, and the less you love and respect yourself. Shame is toxic. The longer it stays in the body, the longer it wreaks havoc. Feelings of unworthiness and self-loathing become the root cause of many dysfunctions in life.

In fact, according to Helen B. Lewis,[1] who recognized the importance of shame to psychotherapy, shame represents an entire group of emotions, including feelings of low self-esteem, humiliation, belittlement, embarrassment, and stigmatization. Feeling shame often translates into experiences of being:

alienated	insecure
bizarre	intimidated
defeated	odd
defenseless	peculiar
different	powerless
dumped	rebuffed
exposed	rejected
flawed	shy
helpless	stupid
hurt	uncertain
inadequate	unworthy
ineffectual	weak
inferior	

Shame is an internal experience, an internal pain. When you feel it on a toxic level, like I felt mine, it makes you disown yourself and completely disconnect from who you are. It is the ultimate self-rejection. That self-rejection becomes the core of your identity until you heal it. The thing is, you can't heal something you don't acknowledge.

To heal the shame within, it's crucial that you get really honest about what shame exists. My own journey in healing took the courage to speak the truth about what

[1] Helen B. Lewis, *Shame and Guilt in Neurosis* (New York: International University Press, 1971).

I was feeling and had been hiding from myself for my entire life.

When the inner self-loathing reached epic proportions (even though my life seemed "good enough" on the outside), it became time for me to do something about it, and I made a list. I took out my journal and made a long list of everything I'd ever said, done, or experienced that made me sick inside when I thought about it.

Beyond mere mistakes, this was a list of things I'd never told anyone I'd said or done. Just writing it down made me anxious that someone would find out. But I kept writing because I knew there was no other solution. Keeping it inside was only making matters worse. And so I wrote and I wrote, crying the whole time.

It actually felt better seeing it all on paper, as if there were some air that could now circulate. Like opening up the windows in a dusty room after a long winter, it was refreshing.

Then I attempted to share it with a healing practitioner I was working with at the time. She waited patiently on the other end of the line while I stared at my list. It took me a lot of quiet sobbing to read the first line, and lots of crying followed.

The healer just listened and encouraged me to keep going. Then I said the second item on the list, again with lots of quiet sobbing and release of the shame. The third item came more easily, with fewer tears. By the time I was halfway through my list, I could read the shameful moments without tears. I could tell that I was healing myself in real time.

When I was done reading, it was as if I'd handed a lifetime's worth of shame back to where it had come from. It was a purifying experience. I experienced compassion and love for myself that I hadn't felt in a long time. This was a defining moment in my life, and from that moment forward, I changed.

I did a similar exercise recently. This time, I brought a journal to the ocean and wrote, "I am ashamed of . . ." For an hour or more, I allowed myself to go deeper and deeper into realms of shame that I hadn't tapped yet. There was some crying, but not as much as the first time I'd done the exercise. I wrote things I'd never given myself permission to write, things I'd been ashamed of since childhood, things I'd never want anyone to read.

At one point I became really surprised by what I wrote, never having been aware that I had shame around certain things in my life, things that were too unfathomable to share with anyone else. And again, writing it all out on paper felt like a releasing gesture, a surrender. It was as if I were giving it back to the source and I was done with it all.

This process of shining a flashlight in the dark corners and excavating the gunk and the sludge inside was cathartic for me. It allowed me to be kinder to myself, to have more compassion and respect for myself, to love myself as I would a child, and to forgive myself. I could get a glimpse of my own magnificence, buried deep under the gunk. It was as if a ray of light were piercing through the darkened sky.

29. You are the lion

> *"The words 'I am' are potent words;*
> *be careful what you hitch them to."*
>
> —A. L. KITSELMAN

You are not a product of your actions or your words. Instead, you are what you believe to be true about yourself. For years, I based my self-image entirely on the shameful things I'd said and done, not on any of the good things I'd created in my life. I believed I was shameful, and that is how I viewed myself. Yes, I may have been holding it all together on the outside, but on the inside, I felt flawed, apart from everyone else, like damaged goods. The good news, though, is that this is no longer the case.

Your actions and your words do not define you. You define yourself by the beliefs you hold to be true about yourself. In shaping your reality and your life, what matters most is how you see yourself on the inside.

Have you ever seen the image of a kitten looking into a mirror and the reflection staring back at him is a lion? The caption states, "What matters most is how you see yourself." My belief about what really happens for most people is that we experience the opposite. We are in fact lions staring into the mirror and seeing only kittens. Instead of seeing your greatness and how magnificent you are, you see a lesser version.

This is an important distinction because you actually shape your life by what you believe to be true about yourself. How you see yourself on the inside dictates your outcomes because it dictates your actions and habits. Here's what I mean:

If you say and believe:

"I am" someone who struggles through life . . .

"I am" never going to be rich . . .

"I am" fat . . .

"I am" always picking the wrong men and making wrong decisions . . .

. . . then, yes, you are absolutely right.

On the other hand, if you say and believe:

"I am" someone destined to win . . .

"I am" a rich and successful person . . .

"I am" getting thinner every day . . .

"I am" always attracting the right people and opportunities . . .

. . . then, yes, you are absolutely right.

If you believe "Nothing I do ever works," then that belief is exactly what's going to manifest in your life. Think of all those lottery winners who lose everything and more within a short year after their windfalls. It's not necessarily that they can't handle their money. It's most likely that they have the self-images that they don't deserve vast amounts of money. This belief about themselves directs their choices and actions, which then fulfill their self-images.

The good news is you can choose to redefine yourself at any moment. You create beliefs about yourself each time you say the words *I am*. By changing your "I am," you can change yourself. You reprogram your belief system by looking at what you currently believe to be true about you and then turning that around.

Make a list of the "truths" about yourself as you see them right now. Not how you think you should see yourself, but how you really see yourself when no one's watching. By the way, no one needs to see this but you. Be raw and honest with yourself; that's the only way to create a breakthrough.

Now, flip these "truths" around and make a list of new "I am" statements about yourself. It might seem difficult at first, because you may feel like a fraud, as if you're making things up. In essence, that might be the truth at first. But one thing you may not know is that the subconscious mind (where your beliefs about you are lodged) has no choice but to accept any image or thought that is presented repeatedly. It cannot differentiate between what's real and what's imagined.

So if you have even imagined your new "I am" statements, if you keep visualizing them on a regular basis, they will start to become true in your self-image. The minute you begin to feel that they are true, your actions will change and your results will follow.

It worked for me, and it's worked for many of my clients who followed in my footsteps. If you'd like to see an example of how to do the "I am" exercise visually with a mind movie, you can view mine by going to www .EmbraceYourMagnificence.com/resources.

I created this mind movie to upgrade what I thought was possible for myself. At the time, we didn't have a team at the office, we hadn't had a third baby yet, I hadn't connected with certain people featured in my mind movie, and I'd never set foot on a private plane. Many of these things have happened and more since I created this movie in 2008, which I watched incessantly. The images started to burn themselves into my brain and my consciousness. After a while, I actually believed that these things were on their way to me. And because I believed it, the results started showing up.

Remember, you are the lion, not the kitten. You are magnificent. Start believing it.

30. Pretend it's Groundhog Day

"If you're not making mistakes, then you're not doing anything. I'm positive that a doer makes mistakes."

—JOHN WOODEN

Everyone makes mistakes. Without mistakes or failures, improvements are impossible. Yet we deeply judge ourselves when we make mistakes. We are often harsher on ourselves than we would ever be on someone else. That level of criticism affects your confidence, which affects everything else in your life.

A mistake or a failure is actually good in the grand scheme of things. Failure is good. Of course, I don't wish it on you every day, but in healthy, small doses, failure is beneficial.

Here's why. If everything went well all the time, you would never have the opportunity to improve. The goal in life is for you to continually get better. One of the best ways to grow is to fail, even though it doesn't feel good while it's happening.

Negative experiences are good because they allow us to get better, to learn, and to improve. It's only a mistake if you don't learn from it. If you learn from it, a negative experience is like the grain of sand that enters an oyster. From it, the oyster creates a pearl.

Speaking personally, I've made many mistakes in my life and have experienced failure, big and small, many times. But here's what you must remember—mistakes only stay failures if you don't learn from them. Growth happens when you learn from your mistakes. If you wallow in your failures and do nothing about them, you do not grow.

There's a process I call "Groundhog Day" that has helped me take the self-criticism and judgment out of my mistakes and turn them into something useful. I call it Groundhog Day because of the movie starring Bill Murray that came out many years ago. Remember how Bill Murray's character has to relive the same day over and over again? At first, he goofs off, plays games, and doesn't use the situation to his advantage. Toward the end of the movie, knowing all that went wrong previously and learning from his mistakes, he is able to perfect what he has to do to win over his love interest.

I've used this concept in my life, in my business, and with my husband and children. It is one of the reasons why things keep getting better and better in my life, because it's an active process that I engage in.

I invite you to apply the Groundhog Day concept to all that you do in your life. After anything that you experience, good or bad, I recommend that you write down the answers to the following three questions:

1. What about this event worked well?

2. What about this event didn't work well at all?

3. Knowing what you know now, if you had to do it all over again the next day (that's the Groundhog Day reference), what would you do differently so that the event became a success?

When you can document and learn from each event, you can create a set of personal rules so that you can create success in the future. When looking at the failures, this process not only helps you improve but also shifts your perception from "bad" to "building block," giving you confidence that you'll be that much more prepared the next time something similar happens.

31. The big reveal

"There's a well-known quote, 'the truth sets you free.' It's a very liberating thing—when you say this is who I am warts and all and then you can just get on with life. It's amazing."

—GERI HALLIWELL

In my life, keeping things looking perfect on the outside was a brutal coping mechanism to protect myself from my shame and feelings of inadequacy. I had to keep the image going so that people would think that I was a good person, despite the fact that I didn't always feel that way inside. Within, I was feeling a lot of pain. There were a lot of truths brushed under the carpet and hiding in the closet.

What I never realized is that it takes an enormous amount of mental energy to keep up a facade. It's a full-time job, in addition to everything else that you've got going on in your life! And this game of always trying to cover up the blemishes is tiring.

I realized that, in the same way I gained freedom by speaking the truth about my shameful moments, the way to gain freedom around other things in my life was to tell the truth about them, too. Speaking the truth about your pain is one of the hardest things to do when you're trying to keep up appearances, but I've realized that this can set you free.

If you're afraid of telling the truth about a particular thing, then it's probably the one thing you must eventually reveal. Speaking it will set you free in a way you've never felt before. To heal fully and become the powerful and magnificent person that you feel you are called to be, you must become willing to look into your pain and feel what you haven't wanted to feel before. It's time to reveal the truth.

I always think of then-candidate Barack Obama revealing some things that his political opponents might have gladly used against him in his books, *Dreams from My Father* and *The Audacity of Hope*. By making these revelations, he put everything on the table, and no one could blame him for hiding anything. What a strategic move this was, even before he campaigned for the presidency.

I had a shameful secret for many years, in fact, most of my life. And if there was one thing that I didn't want anyone to find out, it was that sometimes I drank compulsively to quell the anxiety I had about my feelings of inadequacy. It happened whenever I was in a situation in which I really wanted to be liked, such as a party with new friends or a dinner with close friends. I wanted to feel as though I belonged, after a lifetime of feeling like I'd never belonged. I would get really anxious, and instead of having a socially acceptable amount of wine, I would drink heavily.

Something would come over me, and I would be out of control. I drank double or triple the amount I would normally drink, and said and did things I deeply regretted the next day. People may have thought that I just drank too much sometimes, but I knew deep inside that the behavior was uncontrollable. I had great shame about it. In fact, I had more shame about the overdrinking and the compulsion around it than I did about the anxiety of not belonging. This created a cycle of shame that led me to drink even more to numb my pain.

One day, I realized that the suffering and self-abuse I was experiencing were just too painful. For years I had beaten myself up the day following an event because of what I'd said or done the night before. I knew it wasn't the alcohol itself that was the cause. The anxiety and the self-loathing based on past shame were the causes of my binges.

And so I told the truth. First to one person, then to my husband, and then to a roomful of 350 people who attended one of my Mind-set Retreat workshops. I was onstage talking about this very thing, speaking the truth and how it sets you free, and I received a strong, intuitive hit that this was the time to release my darkest truth and be freed from it.

I hesitated onstage. There was risk there. These were my clients, my future clients, colleagues, my entire staff, and my husband. Some of these people didn't know me, and some knew me very, very well and would never have suspected.

Then I decided to go for it, in courage and with faith that I would be fine. Calmly, I told them that I was about to reveal something that I'd only told to two people. I laid it all out there. I talked about my shame, my feelings of lack of control stemming from my childhood experiences, my anxiety, and my coping mechanism.

I talked about my destructive behaviors, and I talked about the process that I've gone through to heal the feelings of not being good enough. I shared how healing my lack of self-worth helped me alleviate the compulsion, and that although I still enjoy wine, the compulsion is not there anymore. I revealed my greatest, most shameful secret to hundreds of people at once, and there it was. I left it all on the stage.

I left for a scheduled break, went straight into the green room with my husband, and cried and cried on his shoulder. The release valve had finally been opened, and I let all my years of shame come out.

The result was astonishing, something I'd never expected. Not only did I feel the most free that I've ever felt in my life but the outpouring of unconditional love, respect, and compassion from the crowd was indescribable. It was almost as if I'd given every one of them the permission and courage to speak their own truths. By revealing the one thing I never wanted anyone to know, I felt more accepted than I ever had in my life.

Do I recommend getting on the rooftop and airing all your dirty laundry for the world to see, or getting on your own stage and telling your secret to hundreds of people at once? Not necessarily. That was my journey. It started with one person I trusted, and then another. I did it only when I felt safe, and I knew that it was going to be a sacred reveal.

Trust your intuition. When it feels right, speak your truth. In all the instances that I've articulated my greatest resentments, failures, and truths, I have received freedom, compassion, and love in exchange. The blossoming can only happen when you decide that putting all your energy into keeping your secret is no longer bearable.

The result is one of the most beautiful feelings of freedom and purity you'll experience.

32. The competition is over

"It's not people who resent successful people; it's resentful people who resent sucessful people."

—BO BENNETT

We get in our own way by feeling that we don't measure up, we're not good enough, and we are somehow inferior to others. The biggest fuel we add to that fire is competing with and comparing ourselves with others, taking them down the first chance we get.

The fastest way to make sure you don't attract good things into your life is to resent and criticize others who have those good things. If you say you want to be successful in your life, but then you resent successful people, you will not attract the opportunities that would make you successful.

I recently read a special edition of a newsmagazine on the topic of Mother Teresa. The issue spanned her lifetime, work, and legacy, and also described one of her biggest critics, a man who spent a lot of his energy defaming her over the years. Not knowing him, I can only guess that he had unexpressed feelings of inadequacy. The only way he could feel better about himself was to take somebody else down.

How many times has someone you know said that he wanted to be wealthy, and in the next sentence said how unfair it is for professional athletes to get multimillion-dollar contracts? How about someone wishing she could manage her weight better, then criticizes a celebrity for having "that body"?

Instead of resenting people for having what you want, it's time to celebrate their accomplishments and rejoice for them.

When I opened my own business, I overcame some obstacles and, after a while, began doing well enough by most people's standards. However, I grew increasingly bitter watching colleagues who'd started their own businesses at about the same time I did grow their businesses much faster than I was growing mine. The more I became fixated on this internal competition, the more frustrated I became, and the more I envied them. I'd catch myself making snide comments and, in the same breath, wishing I could have what they had. The more I did this, the more I experienced a lag in my own success.

I'm not the only one. If you're honest with yourself, you too have probably criticized, compared, or silently competed against someone who is doing well. Sometimes we compete with people in our family, our closest friends, people in the community, fellow students, and even celebrities we've never met. I've discovered that when you compete in this way, and especially when you criticize what you simultaneously want to have, it's the criticism that has the most effect. What you want actually gets repulsed by you rather than attracted to you.

The longer I whined and had negative feelings toward those I wanted to emulate, the less tangible my results became. The day I finally started celebrating my friends' accomplishments, looking for ways to congratulate them (even if it was just me in my little office by myself), is the day the opportunities came. That's when my income grew, first by a little and then by leaps and bounds.

Catch yourself in the act of competing and making snide remarks. Bless others from afar for showing you that success is possible and it can be done. Be grateful to them for finding and showing you that path. Celebrate them for their successes, knowing that when you celebrate someone else, you get inspiration for yourself.

Acknowledge them for their hard work and dedication. If a friend is better at something than you are, celebrate her and ask her for advice on how to improve. There are things you do better than your friend ever will. The key is to end the competition. Redirect the unhealthy competition on the outside to a healthy one on the inside, with yourself. Strive to improve and expand.

33. The Elusive Carrot

*"Why are some successful people happy and others not? . . .
The happy individuals look at life from one perspective;
the unhappy look at life from another."*

—DAN SULLIVAN

We often get in our own way by not recognizing or celebrating our own successes. We forget how much we've accomplished or how much abundance we have in our lives because we're so quick to move on to the next thing. Some people go so far as to focus obsessively on the 2 percent that's not going well, as opposed to putting their attention on the 98 percent that is going well.

Keeping your focus on what's new and good, as well as on what you have accomplished, is important because it gives you a feeling of confidence. It becomes proof that if you were able to do one thing, then surely you can do another. It requires that you acknowledge and celebrate your accomplishments, significant and otherwise. But for many people, this is easier said than done.

One of the exercises I share with my clients is the Elusive Carrot concept. Imagine that you have a headband on, and there is a long stick strapped to it, hanging right out in front of you about a yard. Next, imagine that at the end of that stick is a carrot. The carrot is your goal in life, or something big that you really want. It's the nature of things, human nature, that as you go forward toward that goal (the carrot), the carrot advances by the same amount, every time.

When we accomplish something, most of us forget to celebrate. And so we also forget to acknowledge our hard work or the great things we have, focusing instead on what we don't have yet. When you measure your accomplishments against the ideal, that Elusive Carrot, you never feel satisfied. It's never good enough, no matter how hard you've worked or how much you've accomplished.

Therefore, you're never good enough. When you measure your accomplishments by looking forward to the always-advancing ideal, you always fall short. This creates feelings of disappointment, depression, hopelessness, frustration, and resentment.

But really, this is just a matter of perspective. If I were to ask you to measure your successes another way, your feelings could change instantaneously. Instead of measuring forward, begin to measure backward. Look at where you were a year ago or ten years ago. List exactly where you were then. List where you are now. The likelihood is you've made much progress.

- How has your life improved in the past 12 months?
- What do you do easily now that you once thought was impossible?
- What have you accomplished this year that you couldn't have accomplished three years ago?
- What is one outcome you experienced this year that would have been inconceivable before?
- What are your results this year, compared with your results last year at this time?

Comparing your results against the Elusive Carrot is an inaccurate measuring stick because you'll always fall short, which means you will always feel not good enough.

The frustration of the Elusive Carrot causes many people to numb out their feelings of inadequacy with coping mechanisms.

- Chronic TV watching
- Eating junk or "comfort" food
- Excessive alcohol consumption
- Excessive eating or bingeing
- Excessive shopping

- Gambling
- Gossiping
- Overworking
- Taking drugs

Conversely, when you measure your successes backward, against where you were before, an entirely different set of feelings shows up. You feel optimistic, confident, hopeful, satisfied, surprised, and appreciative. You take pride in your accomplishments.

In this scenario, there is no need to cope. In fact, you feel as if you're on top of the world, ready to take on the next challenge with confidence. It is all a matter of perspective.

Chapter 6

Forgive All Others

34. Better out than in

"If you don't cry above, you'll cry below."

—SOUTH AFRICAN SAYING

I have never seen anyone benefit from holding on to anger and resentment. When we feel we have been wronged, we are angry because we feel we are right and want to be made to feel right by others, especially the offending person.

Unexpressed emotions turn toxic in the body. It is becoming more accepted in mainstream thought that unexpressed emotions are similar to pollutants in the air and contaminants in our food. Imagine your unresolved feelings and unspoken truths are like chemicals poured into your body day after day. Your feelings of anger, grief, pain, shame, and guilt can become rage, which equals a high level of internal toxicity.

Your unexpressed emotions affect you on a cellular level and stay with you until you release them. Even though you generate new cells every day, new organs every few months and years, energetically, your cells carry forth the emotions that haven't been released and will continue to do so until you speak your truth and get the emotions out. Holding on to anger may make you feel "right," but the more you keep it inside or push it down, the more you are allowing your body to absorb that anger. This is emotional toxicity.

Toxicity holds you back. Once you release the anger and speak your deepest truth, you bring healing in—not only on an emotional level but also on a physical level. You must take control of the situation and reverse it. This is an active role. Instead of being in the passive place of victimhood, it's time that you act to free yourself from the sickness of resentment and anger.

There is an expression: "Better out than in." This is true for emotions that have not had an opportunity to be expressed. You must let yourself feel that which you have not wanted to feel before, and then release it. It's the only way to prevent the negative emotion from lingering and controlling your life. You must express your truest, deepest emotions. Get them out. Express yourself, even if the person who inspired the emotion never hears it.

It is possible for you to hang on to your anger for years while the person who caused you this feeling is not even thinking about you. That person is doing his or her own thing and isn't aware that you are still reliving the incident. Meanwhile, you have been trapped in a spiral of resentment that makes you feel more angry as time goes on.

After college, I once again made a very poor choice in selecting a boyfriend. My intuition told me that he was going to be trouble, but I chose to ignore the guidance and started a relationship with him. The signs were everywhere, from the way he treated his mom to the controlling way he had when he was with me. My friends told me he was bad news. Instead of listening, I rebelled and went with him anyway.

Things got worse. He became abusive. After a year, I was trying to leave him and he knew it. He thought I was dating someone at the office. He began stalking me, calling my home dozens of times an hour. I went to the police to get a restraining order.

The same day, he did the lowest of the low, tapping right into my greatest fear—public humiliation. He handwrote a note about me and faxed it to everyone at the corporation I worked for in New York City. More than a thousand people worked there. Imagine every fax machine, dozens and dozens of them, printing how I used men for money, I had sexually transmitted diseases, I was a thief, and I broke people's hearts. Colleagues, bosses, and heads of departments took me quietly to the side and, heads hung low, showed me the faxes.

I don't think I can even fully express today how deep the shame was, how horrifying the humiliation was. It seemed as though my world was over. It didn't even matter what he had written; it was beyond my comprehension that a human being could do this to someone else. I was enraged. I was broken.

Even though I quickly moved on to another more stable relationship, every time I thought about him and what he had done, my blood would boil. I felt powerless over my emotions. When talking about him, I would say that if I ever saw him again, I would physically hurt him to the degree that he emotionally hurt me.

But then one day, I heard from a family member that my previous boyfriend was happily living with his new girlfriend. He was completely unfazed by what he'd done to me. I was even more angry, but now I was angry at the fact that I had been bitter and incredibly resentful while he was having a grand time in his own life.

That's when I realized that enough was enough. I decided to put an end to my spiral of resentment. I wrote him a letter and expressed everything I felt about him, without censoring anything. I let it all out and allowed myself to get in touch with what had been buried inside—not just that one incident, but all the emotional, physical, and sexual abuse I had allowed to develop in the relationship.

I went deep. After an hour or so, and lots of sobbing, there was nothing left to write. I'd said it all. For the first time in years, I felt surprisingly calm about him and everything that had happened. It was as if the darkness and bitterness that had filled me so completely gave way to light and brightness. There was a quiet emptiness, and it felt good.

I never sent the letter. There was no need. My only purpose for it was to heal myself.

I've done this same exercise many times since, with different people and situations, and each time it's been very helpful and cathartic for me, especially when coupled with energy work and alternative healing modalities.

The biggest lesson I have learned is that you must express it, even if the other person never hears it. It's the only way to prevent it from remaining toxic in your life. Get it all out.

For me, journaling, energy work, and talking about my feelings with an intuitive healer have been the most successful avenues of expression. Perhaps for you, expressive movement and other healing modalities will work. It doesn't matter what you do; find what works for you and make the effort to get it all out of your system.

35. Their hurt runs deep

"Don't be in such a hurry to condemn because he doesn't do what you do, or think as you think or as fast. There was a time when you didn't know what you know today."

—MALCOLM X

Once you've gotten out all the pain and you have that sense of relief, seek the path of forgiveness. Look for compassion and, dare I say it, even love. It seems crazy to think about having compassion for and being willing to forgive someone who did something really terrible to you. And yet this is what helps you truly get past what happened and be able to benefit from it on a soul level.

How do you have compassion for someone who's hurt you so badly or trespassed against you? Understand that the people who say or do things against you have likely been victimized in the past. Research has shown that most people who emotionally abuse others have been emotionally abused themselves. A person who shames another is someone who has been shamed. A person who physically harms another is someone who has been physically harmed.

If you look at it this way, you will understand that every aggressor was once a victim, usually as a child. They too are lost, and the likelihood is that they are operating from the fear of a lost child who didn't get enough love. For many, retaliation in whatever form is an act of self-preservation, reenacting what was done to them.

Forgive them for what they've said or done to you. Have compassion for the person who hurt you. Most people are only using the tools they currently have in any given situation. Perhaps if they knew better, they would do better. Forgive them for their shortcomings and the limited tools they have. Try to see it from their points of view. Everyone thinks they're right, without exception, and yet how could that be possible?

In September 2001, I was living in New York City with Derek, my then fiancé, soon-to-be husband. He worked in the World Trade Center. When the planes hit the Twin Towers, we lost our best friend and many other people we knew, as so many others did. Countless children lost their parents, families were ruptured, and hearts were broken.

Yes, I was incredibly grateful that Derek was able to run out of Tower Two as the buildings were engulfed in flames, but I was still angry. It was a raw time. That night and for the week that followed, I found myself reading newspapers I'd never normally read—those with alarmist headlines and angry stories that made me feel more angry by the minute and even more fearful about the future.

And then one day, it hit me like a ton of bricks. Those who had planned 9/11 so meticulously thought they were right. They felt entitled to their actions, even happy about the ensuing results, because they too were angry. They were resentful at what they thought the world was turning into, and they were blaming us.

They were probably trained to hate and were victims of criticism themselves. They had been victimized just as much as they had just victimized others. It had been modeled for them.

When I realized this, only two weeks after 9/11, when the city and our friends were still grieving, I had an instant flash of all-encompassing forgiveness. Clearly, I didn't condone what the attackers had done. I was still incredibly sad and grieving. But I came to realize that my raging anger toward them would not change what had happened. It could not bring back my friends and all those people who'd perished.

I realized that to be free of the anger and fear, I would have to have compassion for those who committed this atrocity. They too must have been victims of hatred and intolerance.

Would my realization have been different if I'd lost Derek that day? I'm not sure. Who's to say? What I know for certain is that at that moment, I realized that deep inside each person who mistreats another resides an inner child with unresolved emotions.

Whether it's that kid who bullied you in school or that guy who angrily cut you off in traffic with his middle finger in the air, understand that they are wounded, frightened children with unresolved emotions. The real healing comes when you can have compassion for them and love them as you would a child, even though their actions may be careless or even heinous and cruel. The quicker you can have compassion for them, the sooner your feelings of anger and resentment get washed away and you are freed from them.

I obviously don't recommend that you send them love letters or support them in their actions. Rather, step into your higher self and, from your soul, love their souls. Not the person necessarily, but his wounded soul. This process of forgiveness and compassion is a sacred process and a courageous one.

That's when you are freed and can make room for attracting peace and abundance into your life.

36. A sheep in wolf's clothes

"We can always find something *to be thankful for, and there may be reasons why we* ought *to be thankful for even those dispensations which appear dark and frowning."*

—ALBERT BARNES

Part of personal growth is growth itself, and growth is never easy. Physically, you've heard of children having growing pains, when their bodies literally ache from growing so quickly. That is a rite of passage for growth: the pain. Letting the old fall away so that the new can come in.

Mentally and spiritually, there is also growth that comes out of the pain you experience from negative events, especially those that are hard for you to forgive. These negative experiences serve a very big purpose— they're part of the process of personal development that is required for you to live up to the massive potential that awaits within you. And the people who are the catalysts for your biggest growth experiences are part of that process.

Whether you realize this or not, the person who wronged you or caused that negative experience was sent to you for your personal and spiritual growth. You were contracted to go through this experience together. At some point in time, your soul and the other's soul made a pact to come down to earth to experience this together and both learn from it.

If you look at it this way, each person who causes you grief or causes you to learn something new about yourself or about life is like an angel, a sheep in wolf's clothes. It certainly doesn't feel like it at the time, especially when someone wrongs you deeply. But if you look for the deeper meaning, the silver lining in each cloud, or the opportunity for growth and healing, you will find it each time.

There are no coincidences. There is a reason for everything in life. Each negative experience is your opportunity to look for the healing and the lesson. It's always there. If you think you can't find it, keep looking. The more someone is a thorn in your side, the bigger the lesson there is.

Whenever there is a breakdown, I have found that there is a breakthrough just around the corner, if I'm willing to look for it and do the work. The work requires me to look within and see my part in something, especially something that I don't like.

- What was my part in it?
- What did I do wrong in this situation?
- What must I learn that I've been unwilling to learn before?

You are being prepared for something bigger, and this was a necessary element of your evolution.

1. Make a list of those who have wronged you in the past.

2. What did you learn from each experience?

3. How has the experience made you stronger and prepared you for something bigger and better?

Once you realize this, you can forgive the perpetrators. They have held a mirror up for your own healing. In fact, you can thank them. "Thank you for-give-ing me the experience that created who I am today. Thank you forgive-ing me the opportunity to heal this." Forgive.

37. A futile attempt

> *"I haven't got the slightest idea how to change people,*
> *but still I keep a long list of prospective candidates*
> *just in case I should ever figure it out."*

— DAVID SEDARIS

Very often, we think that we can change others. Perhaps it's in a relationship, where you don't take someone for who he truly is, but for what he will become after you change him. We're taught that, over time, we can mold another to be our ideal. We make commitments based on that, rather than to the person as is.

Don't attempt to change others; it won't work. I've learned that if you want to influence someone to be different, the only thing you can do is be your most authentic self. When you set out on your own course, you set an example for how you live your life. After that, it's the other person's choice, not yours, whether to follow you in that course of action. If you try to force something onto someone without permission, you will encounter backlash.

A few years ago, I encountered someone who could, through hand analysis and palmistry, help me figure out my life purpose.

This was a life-defining moment for me. Finding out that I am here to be a powerful, innovative spiritual teacher and healer rocked my world. It was as though my whole life, my experiences good and bad, my inclinations, my trials, and my tribulations all finally came together and made sense to me for the first time in my 35 years. I'd found my own version of the Holy Grail.

And so, naturally, I wanted my husband, Derek, to find out his life purpose, as well. I fully expected him to get his own hand analysis and jump on it like I had. Instead, I was met with a lot of resistance from him. I was completely baffled by it, shocked, and angry. I arrogantly complained to him, "How is it possible that I, of all people, am married to someone who doesn't want to know what his life purpose is?"

His reply was always, "I just don't want to. I'm not interested in doing that right now." It got me more incensed each time he said it. The more I tried to push it down his throat, mentioning it to him over and over again, the more resistance I met and the higher the wall got between the two of us on this topic.

Until one day I gave up on trying to get him to do what I wanted him to. I surrendered to my own spiritual path without talking to him about it. I wasn't hiding it. I told Derek that if he ever wanted to talk about it with me, I'd be happy to, but that I wouldn't mention it anymore. And I experienced a wave of relief.

What I hadn't realized is that I was bullying him to make changes. Even though it was against his will at the time, I thought I was right and he was wrong. Right or not, it was absolute arrogance on my part. He had a full life without knowing his life purpose, and here I was trying to tell him that his life was inadequate if he didn't do things my way.

So I left him alone about it. I continued on my own path, read books about the subject, worked with healers to move me along in my journey, and started living my purpose. The more I did, the more successful I became in my business (financially and otherwise), the happier I was, and the more fulfilled I felt in my life.

Then a funny thing happened. Amid our happy, everyday marriage, Derek witnessed how all of this was slowly transforming my life, how happy and fulfilled I was compared with the previous few months. He started getting curious on his own. He picked up the books I had left on his nightstand months earlier and read them.

It was his idea to watch a movie on metaphysics one night, the same movie he'd resisted watching with me in the past. I was shocked. Even when we'd watched it or when he'd read one of the books I'd recommended a long time ago, I kept the same low profile. I didn't say a word and I continued not to push. I let him find his own path as I had found mine.

Today, Derek lives and breathes this information with me. He's had his hand analysis done (it was his idea) and is living his life purpose. The key lesson for me was that it was his choice. The only way to change someone is to not try. Just be yourself, do what feels right for you, and let the proof be in the pudding. Be an inspiration rather than a dictator. If you do anything else, you are being a bully.

At the same time, understand that it will not always happen like this. Sometimes people will never see it your way. I've tried sharing books and concepts that have changed my life with family members. The books were never read, the ideas never embraced. At first, I was frustrated. I saw myself as providing a solution to what was ailing them, and it was not received well. Now I know that it's okay. I was being bossy and arrogant.

Understand that they have their own journeys, and you have yours. You must be true to yourself and let them be true to themselves. Remember, their lives are full, even if you think they could be fuller. Stay on your path. If it influences someone positively, then so be it. If not, then you weren't supposed to be the person to influence them. Honor them for who they are right now.

38. What you resist, persists

"Whenever you are experiencing discontentment or unhappiness, there is something you are resisting. All suffering is caused by non-acceptance of what is . . . You suffer when you want things to be different from how they are. What you resist persists."

—RICHARD PATERSON

When you are presented with something—a thought, a feeling, a struggle, or a situation—that shows up again and again, you have free will to take action or not. But if something comes up again and again, there is a reason for it. It is presenting itself because you need it, because on a subconscious level you have asked for it as an opportunity for advancement or healing.

Recognize that when things come up, it's an opportunity to heal them. Otherwise, the same story will come up over and over until you resolve it.

In most cases, it's not the thought or experience that's causing you pain; it's the fact that you're resisting the learning. The experience and your feelings around the experience are the gateway for you to learn and heal something about yourself. Until you learn the lesson and heal the wound, the opportunity for growth (pain, discomfort) will continue to show up. The more you say yes to what you've resisted, the less you will suffer and the more you will find contentment.

Instead of getting down on yourself when something bad happens, look for the meaning in it. Seek out the opportunity to speak the truth. Be willing to do things differently and experience a breakthrough.

When something comes up that makes you feel uncomfortable, acknowledge it and know that there is nothing wrong with it. Rather, you are being given an opportunity to heal something within or change something about yourself for your highest good and the highest good of all. When you embrace the situation and step into the learning that is being made available to you, the thing you're struggling with dissolves very quickly.

Ask yourself:

- What am I being asked to learn about myself?

- What am I being called to heal within myself?

- What am I being guided to change?

39. You're not their healer

"If people don't like you, that's their bad taste."

—TAB HUNTER

It's an unrealistic expectation to want to please everyone in your life. Not everyone can be pleased. Some people go to great lengths to try and make sure everyone likes them because they want to feel good about themselves, but the reality is, you can't make everybody like you.

As I mentioned earlier, even Mother Teresa had staunch critics, and at least one person made it his task in life to take her down. Why are people critical of even the most benevolent personalities? My belief is that they want to have something to feel passionate about. There are people who feel better, who find that passion, in taking other people down.

Some people will like you; some won't. It's just chemistry, part of the sacred contract you have with them. It's not personal.

When I studied nutrition prior to opening my first business, a holistic nutrition practice, I was assigned a series of student clients to work with to practice my consulting skills. I'd never met them, but I was excited to help them incorporate more whole foods into their diets and heal some of their emotional wounds and personal challenges so they would be better suited to help their own clients.

I was assigned 20 student clients. I thought I had a great relationship with each of them. Then, in one week, three of them went to the head of the counseling program and expressed interest in being switched to another counselor. I was devastated. My manager at the school questioned me. What was I doing wrong?

What was I not giving them that another person would? What was I doing to them that they wanted to switch? My confidence spiraled downward.

I tried to get answers, but nothing came. Until I spoke to someone outside the situation, and she offered a word of advice. "Fabienne, nothing's wrong with you. You're simply not their healer."

No matter what I did to please them, to make them happy, it wouldn't have worked. One felt that my strong boundaries ruffled her feathers. Another didn't like the fact that I hadn't ever been as overweight as she was currently and therefore couldn't speak from my experience. The third simply resonated better with another counselor, who had a lot in common with her.

All of these things were outside my control. I was who I was, and despite the fact that I was a good health counselor and that I cared for them, we weren't meant to be working together. They had a sacred contract to work with someone else.

Not everyone will like you. Some will leave you. When I realized this, what they felt about me no longer hurt me. It was no longer about me, but about their journey, and their journey was not meant to be with me.

This was a relief. It didn't matter anymore, and I could move on, knowing that I was a healer to the others who were working with me then and others who are working with me today.

40. They fear losing you

"When we see others beginning to live their authentic selves, it drives us crazy if we have not lived out our own. Individuals who are realized in their own lives almost never criticize others. If they speak at all, it is to offer encouragement."

—STEVEN PRESSFIELD

When you shine your inner light into the world by expressing yourself to the fullest, you will likely come up against some opposition. As you are more and more yourself in your life, fully self-expressed, fully embracing yourself and your gifts, you will receive pushback from others, sometimes those who are closest to you.

Wouldn't you think that those who love you the most would be the most supportive? That's not always the case. As you grow, as you become more authentic and aligned with who you really are and what you're here to do, you will bring out envy in others. Most important, you will bring out their fears.

You may experience the envy of others because you are doing something they haven't given themselves permission to do. Those witnessing your transformation are often still locked in their own self-imposed prisons of inauthenticity. They are unable to be fully who they are or to take risks as you did. It pushes their buttons when you do just that.

When you step into doing what you want to do in life, some people will fear losing you. The way you used to be is familiar to them, and now you are changing the rules of your relationships. They may resent you for that.

When you change, it threatens the status quo. It rocks the boat. There are many people who would rather be comfortable than do what their heart tells them. When you make changes for the better, some people will challenge you to stay the same as you were before, coming up with every logical reason why the old way was better or safer.

I mentioned the fear attached to this earlier: it's the fear of being inadequate. They've been holding on to living a mediocre life and surrounding themselves with people who enable them to stay mediocre. When you step out to do something extraordinary, it confronts their ways of thinking and their beliefs of what life is supposed to be.

Have you ever seen someone lose five or ten pounds, and then witnessed how that person's friends will suddenly suggest going out for pizza and ice cream? They'll say, "Oh, just one more slice of pizza!" When the successful dieter refuses, she is met with, "What are you, too good for us now?"

A few years ago, I attended some personal growth and development workshops on evenings and weekends. I knew that I had a lot of emotional baggage. Instead of going through what I thought would be many years of therapy to unravel the baggage, I decided to work on my stuff all at once, over the period of a few weekends.

After great results, I invited some key friends and family members to consider joining me in the training. I was met with great resistance and criticism. They tried to warn me, telling me I was making a mistake and no good would come from this. There was no way they would consider trying it for themselves. I was shocked. I had gained so much from this training, and I wanted to share it with them. Who doesn't want to share a good thing?

Years later, I joined friends for dinner after a weekend training on the mind-set required to make a million dollars. It had been a fantastic weekend, and I'd learned so much. But at dinner, my friends ribbed me for doing something they thought was pie in the sky. I knew better then, and I simply smiled and said, "Watch me do it."

In the years since, I've done it several times. They are now quiet about my success in business and my income and have since asked me for advice.

As you step out of the ordinary and into something different, something that requires a risk or a change in status quo, you take on the role of the person who will challenge the comfort zone of others. You will make others feel that they too must make a change or be left in the dust. Feelings of inadequacy come up. It's almost as if you are holding a mirror up for them and saying, "When will you do something for yourself?" It doesn't matter whether or not you are actually saying that; it's a perception others may have.

If people resent your success, it's because they are resentful about not being in the same place. It underlines their own inadequacies. Therefore, it has nothing to do with you or what they think of you.

You cannot take it personally, whether it's someone you know or someone you've never met before. Their reactions are not really about you. Their reactions are about them and how they respond to you. That is something you cannot control and will never be able to control.

If you're doing the right thing, living with integrity, and doing the best you can in life, then the rest is up to them. Bless them. Do not take it personally. Keep moving in the direction of your dreams.

Chapter 7

Understand There Is a Bigger Plan for You

41. The universe is strategic

"Look in your own heart. Unless I'm crazy, right now a still small voice is piping up, telling you as it has ten thousand times, the calling that is yours and yours alone. You know it. No one has to tell you."

—STEVEN PRESSFIELD

Even though many people go through life feeling discouraged and believing they don't have a purpose, nothing could be further from the truth. No matter who you are, you have a purpose for being here. You are part of the whole reason for being. In fact, the universe has plans for you that dwarf anything you have imagined so far.

Most people play way too small in life, believing they don't have what it takes to do great or important things in service of others. But because God is your Creator and you can't outcreate God, know that there is a sacred plan for you, too, a bigger dream for you than you could ever have for yourself.

Before you were born, your soul made a contract with other souls. You cooperated with the universe to create this plan and reason for your life. Because this plan, your purpose, was designed in cooperation with the universe, it is bigger than you realize right now. Because of its participation, the universe has a vested interest in you reaching your life purpose. As such, you have access to all the resources you will ever need within the realm of creation, anytime of the day or night, for as long as you need them to achieve your purpose.

You have free will. Even though you have this purpose and the help of your Creator in achieving these goals, it's up to you to want to do it. You have free will to not follow your purpose, to sabotage your plans, to head in the wrong direction, to get in trouble, or to use a different way to get there.

This means that you must first make the commitment to live your life purpose, even if you don't quite know what it is yet. When you've made that decision, the universe will conspire with you to make it happen. But not without your decision.

The writer W. H. Murray expressed this sentiment beautifully in *The Scottish Himalayan Expedition*:

Until one is committed, there is hesitancy, the chance to draw back, always ineffectiveness. Concerning all acts of initiative (and creation) there is one elementary truth, the ignorance of which kills countless ideas and splendid plans: that the moment one definitely commits oneself, then Providence moves, too. All sorts of helpful things happen that would never otherwise have occurred. A whole stream of events issues from the decision, raising in one's favor all manner of unforeseen incidents and meetings and material assistance, which no man could have dreamed would have come his way. I have learned a deep respect for one of Goethe's couplets: "Whatever you can do, or dream you can, begin it. Boldness has genius, power, and magic in it."

By saying yes to your life purpose, you become a warrior for the universe. You transform yourself into a vessel through which good things are done for the greater whole. When you do, you will feel an all-encompassing meaning and fulfillment for your life. You will recognize the magnificence that comes by virtue of being an empty vessel for Source to do its work through you.

From this place of service, you get rewarded in ways you could never imagine. When you follow your purpose, all the meaning, fulfillment, money, recognition, security, abundance, appreciation, and everything you were seeking before naturally come to you.

The more you serve your purpose, the more the universe rewards you. The more you align with your purpose in service of others and the greater whole, the more opportunities you receive. You are literally being rewarded for a job well done.

Make the commitment to say yes to your purpose. Then be open to receiving more good in your life than you've ever experienced, realized, or imagined before.

42. Share your brownies

"You are not the momentary whim of a careless creator experimenting in the laboratory of life . . . You were made with a purpose."

— OG MANDINO

We're all here to be of service, in our own special way and in a big way. You see, each one of us came into the world to contribute, to serve others. We've each been given specific talents, unique abilities and skills, ways of being and ways of doing, and life experiences (both good and not so good) that have contributed to the whole package of who we are. None of this was by accident. It was all for a purpose, one that is much greater than you may be able to see right now.

I call it sharing your brownies.

Imagine that you are alone in your kitchen while the rest of your friends and family are in your living room. Quietly, secretly, you've been baking up a batch of ooey, gooey, chocolaty brownies. As they're about to come out of the oven, a close friend pokes her head into the kitchen and says, "Something smells really good! What are you making in there?"

Imagine that your response is, "None of your business! I'm not doing anything. Go back to the living room."

Puzzled, your friend leaves. You take the tray of brownies out of the oven. Once they've cooled a bit, you cut up them up into perfect squares and stack them beautifully on a round platter. You pick up the tray. But instead of taking the platter out to your friends and family who are eagerly waiting for you, you choose to go to the corner of your kitchen and eat all the brownies by yourself—the entire platter, down to the last crumb.

Would you consider that being stingy? Maybe even a little greedy? It's the same thing with your gifts, talents, and unique abilities.

You were given these, along with your personal life experiences (remember, the good ones and also the not-so-good ones), and the combination of all of these things makes up who you are.

You were not given these gifts to squander or to hoard. No—you were given these tools and created exactly as you are for the purpose of making a difference in other people's lives in the way only you can. There is no one quite like you, and there never will be.

This is why I believe that if you don't say yes to your natural inclinations and use them in a big way, you are hoarding these divine gifts. Would you consider that being stingy, too?

I continually tell my clients that it is their divine duty to share their brownies with the world. Otherwise, it is the equivalent of slapping your Creator in the face.

This person you've become, the one who's here to be of service, absolutely must get out of her own way. Use your life to serve in the way only you can serve. This can be through your work, by embracing your creativity, volunteering, teaching, even creating a movement. Most especially if you're in business for yourself, I believe that you must play a much bigger game. Do whatever you can to let yourself be found by the legions of people who need what you provide but don't know about you yet.

Your gifts are meant to be shared—even if you're scared, even if you don't want to, even if you fear failure, or success, or criticism. If you choose not to share your brownies, my belief is you're wasting the gifts that were divinely given to you.

Deep down, we're here for one thing. It doesn't matter what we do for a living, what industry we're in, what our strengths and skills are. Life is about living in a way that matters. When you realize that it's your divine duty to use these skills, and you do so, you begin changing the world.

This might sound a little grandiose at first. But right now as you read this, there are people you could help, people who are tossing and turning in the middle of the night, worried, overwhelmed, frustrated, and not knowing what to do about their particular situations. You currently have the solution to their problems. It is imperative that you help them. With each person you serve, sharing your brownies in a bigger way, you change the world, maybe even in a significant way.

Imagine a placid lake at dusk, with its silvery sheen. It's quiet, not a person in sight. Now imagine dropping a rock into that placid lake. Doing so creates a ripple. That ripple travels farther than the original entry point of the rock.

With each person you help, whether it's through your business, mentoring a disadvantaged child, writing poems, or sponsoring someone in need, you change not only that person's life but also the lives of those around that person.

By virtue of that change, you create a ripple effect that touches spouses, children, co-workers, friends, family members, and so on. All those lives affect other people's lives. Through that one life you've changed, you've affected untold numbers of lives, even if just subtly. And that was just through the first person you helped.

Now imagine throwing a second heavy rock into that placid, silvery lake. More ripples, countless ripples, and an even greater ripple effect with untold lives changed. Imagine dropping 20 rocks into the lake. Imagine 200, 2,000, 200,000 rocks. The ripple effect can be endless.

The more widely you share your brownies, the more you change the world, and the more handsomely you will be rewarded for it—in meaning, in fulfillment, and otherwise.

As a side note, the more people you serve, the more rewarded you are financially, especially if you're in business for yourself. The formula I share with my students for making a lot more money is simple. Please don't underestimate its simplicity, because it is actually pretty profound.

The formula for abundance:

1. Give a lot more value to the marketplace than you're giving now (share your brownies).

2. Do this with a lot more people than you're doing now (play a bigger game).

That's when the universe will reward you with opportunities and financial returns you hadn't expected.

The things you have experienced in your life so far, both the good and the not-so-good things, created who you are today. You can now help others struggling through the same things you've experienced. There are people who are now in the "before" stage of your "before-and-after" story. They need your expertise, experience, and guidance. Use your story, experiences, lessons, talents, and journey to serve them.

Share those brownies. It's your divine calling.

43. Find your way through play

"Find your way through play."

—SAYING ON THE BACK OF A
MAGIC HAT #9 BEER BOTTLE CAP

Finding one's purpose is something that eludes a lot of people. It did me, for a long time. You likely already know what yours is, but you've judged it as not being important enough. Or perhaps others have tainted how you perceive your purpose.

Your life's purpose is something that comes to you so naturally and that you're so good at that you sometimes discount it. It is something you have great passion for, something you get better and better at each time you do it, something that you would do for free all day long for the rest of your life.

Because it comes so naturally to you, you don't feel that you are very qualified. Some people feel that if it's not hard work, it's not worth doing.

How do you begin to discover your life purpose? Get curious. Discover what you're naturally drawn to. Look at the books on your bookshelf or nightstand. Ask yourself:

- What books or sections of the bookstore are you always drawn to?

- What moves you to tears in your life?

- What is it that you would feel remiss about if you didn't accomplish it in this lifetime?

- What is your story?

- What have you been able to accomplish that others would do anything to learn?

- What are your deepest values?

- What do you prize above anything else?

- What makes you feel most fulfilled and gives your life meaning when you do it?

- Think of a moment in your life when time flew by and you didn't see it go. Who were you with? What were you talking about or doing? How were you helping?

A defining moment in my life happened when I opened my first business. I had just left a job in the corporate world. My former assistant was interested in getting nutrition counseling sessions from me but couldn't afford my fees. I needed some administrative tasks done. We decided to trade an hour of filing for an hour of nutrition counseling once a week.

At first, she and I discussed her food choices, and I gave her recommendations on what to increase and what to decrease in her diet. After a few weeks, we noticed that her relationship with her boyfriend was affecting her job, her health, and her self-esteem. She hadn't realized that she deserved better in her life. So I shared some simple principles with her about embracing her magnificence, setting some boundaries, playing a bigger game, and strengthening her spiritual connection.

I could have talked with her about this all day long, at no charge, day after day. She was really moved by our conversations and made significant improvements in many aspects of her life as a result of our weekly sessions. She upgraded her image of herself and what she thought was possible for her. She set new standards and boundaries, ended her relationship with her boyfriend, found a better job, and got healthy.

Most important, she began to love herself and strengthen her spiritual connection. And the best part for me was that each of us felt that we were getting the better end of the exchange. What I did with my former assistant is what has ended up being my life purpose. I still get great joy from doing it for free all day long.

Do what you're good at, what comes naturally to you. Do what feels good and helps or serves others. Follow your bliss. That's your life purpose, and people who follow this are successful.

44. God doesn't call the qualified

"I believe that you're great, that there's something magnificent about you. Regardless of what has happened to you in your life, regardless of how young or how old you think you might be, the moment you begin to think properly, this something that is within you, this power within you that's greater than the world, it will begin to emerge. It will take over your life. It will feed you, it will clothe you, it will guide you, protect you, direct you, sustain your very existence. If you let it."

—DR. MICHAEL BECKWITH

Often, I encounter people who believe that they don't have what it takes to fulfill a big purpose being of service to others, as I didn't in the beginning. They feel inadequate; they are scared that they don't know enough and that they are not enough to do big things.

That's not the case. You are here to do great things, just by virtue of who you are and what you've experienced so far. You didn't experience all you've experienced for it to go to waste. There is a purpose for it, and all of it is useful—all of it. But if you examine the reasons why people don't make the decision to live their purpose on a very big level, most of the time, you find that it's a fear of not being good enough and not having what it takes.

Let's be honest. Sometimes you may be scared that you're not good enough or qualified enough to reach that big goal, so you don't even try. In fact, you don't know how "it" would ever happen, you don't "see it," and, therefore, you don't go after "it."

Have you ever felt on the verge of something big, that the next level is just within your reach, and at the same time wondered if you have what it takes to make it happen, if you can actually handle it? There was a point in time when I observed this among colleagues, students, and clients of mine.

I wondered, "Why is everyone around me afraid of the next level? Why not just do what it takes?" Well, after some reflection, it dawned on me that my clients were essentially holding up a mirror for me. Deep inside, I'd been feeling the same fear of leaving my current comfort zone for something much bigger.

Things had been going great in my business, and yet I kept having this nagging feeling that the next big level was about to show up. (Speaking now, from hindsight, it was right in front of me.) At the same time, it seemed like I was being asked by the universe to really step up my personal growth: "Healer, heal thyself."

I saw how I had to surrender even more to what was possible for me in order to teach others about how to play a bigger game in their businesses and their lives. Several experiences came up in which my old ways of being were proven no longer valid, especially not for a business that was about to grow dramatically—to triple in size in one year, although I didn't know it at the time.

Normally, I'm known for taking a no-excuses approach to clearing out anything that's getting in the way. But this time, the obstacles were more difficult to overcome than usual. I questioned whether I was willing to do what it would take, whether I had the courage to go really big.

Then my good friend Carolyn sent me a copy of the movie *The Moses Code*, saying knowingly, "This is what you need, Fabienne." By Chapter 5 of the DVD, I had broken down and sobbed at length at my desk. Not from sadness, but in response to the humbling potential of what is possible for anyone, for my clients, and even for me.

Although there were many useful nuggets in the movie, the prevailing message for me was simple: we all have a destiny for greatness. And, as the film says, it can be a little scary to tackle an idea so big. The calling for our next stage of evolution (and success) is always upon us. There is a journey that you are being asked to take, something very big.

But what was also pointed out in the movie is that, instead of embracing the journey, we often say to ourselves, "Who am I to do this? I don't have what's required. I'm not enough for that."

The truth is that we must come to the realization that we are all being called to something great. It's okay that we are not presently able to deliver that destiny. But we grow into it if we say yes to the challenge. That's all it takes. Then everything we need is given to us.

Here's a quote from the film that really moved me and got me to understand what was going on for me then. "God does not call the qualified; He qualifies the called through the 'yes.'"

The important thing I realized is that the you who originally says yes to the calling is not the same you who will reach that destiny. We're constantly evolving and unfolding based on our ability and willingness to say, "Yes, I'll go on that journey."

When you say yes when called and challenged to reach the next level, the entity that called you also qualifies you over time. When you say yes to the next big level in your life, you begin to receive the resources, the skills, the mentor, the employee with the right contacts, the guidance, the money—everything begins to show up. You then change and grow into the person able to deliver the destiny. You have been qualified.

The message that moves me still today is that you don't need to be enough to say yes to your destiny. The minute you step in and agree to the challenge, God will step in and qualify you over time. There's nothing to do but say yes and be willing to do the next right thing that is presented.

In this way, you can do anything, because the universe works directly with you to make sure you transform into the person who will be qualified to deliver the destiny. All you have to do is say yes.

45. The scavenger hunt of life

"Faith is taking the first step even
when you don't see the whole staircase."

—Dr. Martin Luther King, Jr.

The universe will gradually prepare you in small ways and then bigger ways. Before you know it, you will be living your life purpose fully. You will not be shown the whole picture of what you are capable of in one fell swoop. At first it will be shown to you in small ways. You will be prepared and qualified in increments: a lesson to learn, a book to read, a friend to meet. All of these will prepare you. The signs will keep showing up, and over time you will become clearer and clearer that you are indeed here for something big.

For many years, I wondered endlessly about my life purpose. I knew deep inside that I was here for something beyond myself, but I didn't know what it was. Now I believe that I had an inkling, and yet I'm glad that I didn't see the whole picture. Otherwise, I would probably have been scared, wondering how I would ever pull it off. Small thinking would have gotten in the way.

Notice your own small thinking as it relates to your big dreams and goals. Is there a way that you might be stopping yourself or putting a hold on your big dreams because you haven't yet figured out how they're going to happen? Is the planner in you squashing the dreamer in you?

I recommend thinking of your life purpose as a scavenger hunt. You receive one clue indicating what you're meant to do next, and only that one clue. You do not receive the second clue until you've successfully found the first item. Then you will get only the second clue, but not the third.

You get just the clue you need, just when you need it. It's actually better that way, because if you got a glimpse of how big your purpose is in this world and how much you're here to actually accomplish, you'd probably be frightened by it. The importance of it would overwhelm you, and you'd crawl back into bed, thinking that there somehow must be a mistake, that "no, not you," that you are not meant to live this destiny.

Instead, I recommend you gather your strength, deny your smallness, and grab hold of the truth about yourself: you can accomplish that big dream. It's not a silly notion. Just the mere fact that you've thought of it means it can be done. The universe would never have allowed you to dream something that it cannot accomplish with you. Otherwise, you wouldn't have gotten the idea.

Forget the how, at least in the beginning. Just go for it. Each "how" and the resource needed at the perfect time will show up exactly when you need it. You will be qualified in time.

Chapter 8

Let Yourself
Be Guided

46. You are never alone

*"You can't connect the dots looking forward; you can only
connect them looking backwards. So you have to trust that the
dots will somehow connect in your future. You have to trust
in something—your gut, destiny, life, karma, whatever. This
approach has never let me down, and it has made
all the difference in my life."*

—STEVE JOBS

Many times, especially when life wasn't going well,
I felt alone. I felt lost, afraid, hopeless, and helpless, asking myself why so many things were going against me. I
kept asking God for a solution, but I felt like I wasn't getting an answer. I felt fundamentally abandoned in my

darkest hour, and this made me angry. It felt like spiritual deprivation or, even worse, spiritual abandonment.

I felt this often. Then one day I experienced a breakthrough that has shaped how I have lived my life ever since. In October 2006, I had taken my business coaching practice, ClientAttraction.com, to a very successful financial level, but my business was at full capacity. I was working all the time, and my husband was begging me not to take on any more individual clients. I was introduced to the business model of working with groups of clients, rather than just one-on-one.

I drew a line in the sand and announced that I was no longer going to accept individual clients. Yet I froze when it came to creating group programs. I found myself in a complete state of inaction. I was overwhelmed and confused. I had a thousand things on my list and didn't have the motivation to do any of them. My income quickly spiraled downward.

At the same time, we'd just purchased an expensive home by the beach based on my ability to make the kind of money I'd been making with a full practice of individual clients. The fear of losing our home paralyzed me even more. I kept waking up in the middle of the night, panicked and covered with sweat. Yet during the day, I let my confusion and fear get in the way of taking action. I felt abandoned and didn't understand why I was not being given direction.

I sought help from an intuitive healer, someone who could channel the universe and my guides. I needed to find out what was going on, why I was being left on my own despite all my requests. And the answer that would change my life came during that session. I was reassured that I was never alone. In fact, I was being guided even now as I felt alone. I was told that my guides were "whispering in my ear" all day long, every day, giving me solutions to the problems that I wasn't able to work out on my own.

Why wasn't I hearing the guidance? Because I was keeping myself too busy. There were so many things on my plate that there was too much mental clutter. I couldn't decipher the guidance I was getting from the list of things I thought I should be doing.

I took out a sheet of paper and wrote down everything that was on my plate at the time, both personal and professional. I was astounded by the sheer number of things that cluttered my mind. In fact, I cried when I saw the dozens and dozens of projects and to-dos I was juggling. No wonder I couldn't hear the guidance. I just had too much in my mind.

My assignment from the universe was to take everything from my shelves—all the reading material, all the things I was working on—and literally put them in the garage. I was instructed to take a 30-day hiatus from reading anything. (I did cheat, though, and continued to read *People* magazine once a week, but I didn't think that was too bad.)

What I discovered from putting a pause button on all the mental clutter and giving myself permission to clear my mind (and my to-do list) is that I started hearing the guidance. I felt myself being pulled in a certain direction, and I saw the signs that had been there for me the whole time, the ones I hadn't been still enough to pay attention to. I realized that the guidance had been there all along, but through the busyness of life and my unwillingness to let go of control, I had missed out on all of it.

Trust that the universe is taking care of you. You are never alone. You are always being guided; you just need to listen. Whether you realize it or not, the universe is always there, showing you the way, ready to help you accomplish any task, and happily leading. You can get guidance effortlessly and gracefully whenever you ask for it and whenever you relinquish the tight fist of control. But you must ask for it.

Surrender to the guidance that will provide you with the opportunities and assistance you need to achieve what you want to achieve.

47. Hold the steering wheel loosely

"If there be anything capable of setting a soul
in a large place, it is this absolute abandonment to God.
It diffuses in the soul a peace which flows as a river, and a
righteousness which is as the waves of the sea."

—FRANÇOIS FÉNELON

When you try to control your life too closely, manipulating circumstances or forcing people to do what you want instead of going with the flow of life, you close yourself off to the vast possibilities of abundance that are available for you. This is hard to hear if you tend to be a controlling person.

There is a reason for everything, especially the stuff you don't want to experience.

What you think you want at a particular time is not always what's best for you over time, or for the greatest good of all involved. You may think you would like a certain relationship or perhaps a new job, but that doesn't always mean it's the best thing for you.

You are being guided. There is a reason for what's happening. Your best interest and the best interests of all involved are also part of the grand plan. You are being led by the universe to events, circumstances, experiences, and people who are placed there for your highest good and the highest good of all, even when it makes no sense at the time. You are being guided all day long, every day.

Yes, there is a plan for your life. But there is also free will, meaning you can do what you want to do and ignore the guidance—as many people do. It's your choice always. You can exercise free will and choose to do the exact opposite of the universe's guidance, which is what I did for a long time. (I still find myself doing this unconsciously sometimes, until I catch myself.)

For many years, I chose to be driven by my inner control freak to have things my way and only my way. In hindsight, this is where the greatest frustrations and disappointments of my life have stemmed from. I am a certifiable control freak about certain things and not at all about other things.

After a lot of personal growth and development work, I now realize that my wanting to control things and the people around me was a direct result of not feeling like I could control my childhood. My parents' divorce and divisive behavior made me feel overwhelmed and out of control.

When my mother packed up our childhood home in Paris and moved my sister and me from France to start a new life in the United States, without telling us or asking for our input, this made me feel even more insecure and unsafe.

Losing my mother in a sudden fatal car accident gave me the sense that I was never on solid ground, that the rug could and would be pulled out from under my feet at any time. So, to feel safe, I created a belief that the only way I could be happy was if I was in control of everything in my life.

This was sound reasoning for a child looking to feel safe, but in adulthood, constantly trying to control every aspect of my life (and of the lives around me) began to create resistance. I wanted to be in a different place in my relationships and my business. I knew that there was something more, but it always seemed out of my reach.

When I couldn't force my life to become what I wanted it to become, I began to ask for guidance, but help didn't seem to be forthcoming. I kept asking, wondering where the guidance was and when my life would get better. I looked at the ceiling in frustration, arrogantly saying, "Why aren't you guiding me? Please help me!" and felt like I wasn't given any response. I became impatient and more lost, overwhelmed, and out of control. I tried to control things even more and hit that same brick wall.

Then the mirror of life showed up once again.

At around this time, I noticed a close friend expressing impatience about why he wasn't getting results as quickly as he wanted in his love life, his health, and his professional development. Every time he was being guided to do something, even if I or others were giving him advice, he ignored it and did just the opposite. He always felt that his way was the best way. Yet as his situation continued, he became even more frustrated and downright angry and judgmental, especially when he witnessed others easily achieving what he so desperately wanted.

Watching him felt like watching a fly continually flying into a glass windowpane, trying to go through it and wondering why it wasn't happening. I realized that if my behavior wasn't working, as my friend's wasn't working, I had better leave my know-it-all, control-freak ways behind and adopt another way of doing things.

I decided to put judgments aside, release my grip, and listen for guidance (in the forms of signs or happy coincidences). I surrendered, accepting that I don't always have the right answer or the best way to do things. I started taking action on what was presented to me.

That's when life started feeling like I was gently canoeing downstream, rather than frantically paddling up the rapids. Things became much easier, and the process of life felt much more graceful. Releasing the control and surrendering to the guidance actually gave me the life I wanted.

One example I often share with my students is when my husband, Derek, and I were living in New York City. We decided to move out of Manhattan to live by the water. Derek worked at an investment bank at the time, and we were looking for a very specific set of circumstances. We knew that we wanted to live in a city that was by the ocean, have a house with a backyard, be on the East Coast, be not too far from his parents' house, and allow Derek to have a five-minute commute, which meant that the city had to have investment banks where he could get a job. So we set our sights on Providence, Rhode Island.

We loved that Rhode Island is known as "the Ocean State," that it had beautiful homes and beautiful beaches with lots of culture and restaurants, and that there were investment banks where Derek could work while providing me with enough networking opportunities to continue building my business. And we loved that we would be very close to Derek's parents' home.

But every time we tried to find a job for Derek in Providence, nothing happened. I even saw resistance on his part. He didn't seem enthusiastic about looking for a job there, and I became upset that we weren't moving forward fast enough. I tried to take control of the job search process, which frustrated him and created even more resistance.

Then one day a friend asked me, "Are you open to having the same things, but in a different city?"

I paused, and instead of coming from the my-way-is-the-only-way style of thinking, I quietly said, "Yes, I am open to that."

That very same week, Derek spoke to a friend at work, letting him know our preferences, and the friend suggested a place that met every single one of our specifications, but that we hadn't even thought of. Everything after that fell into place, like a string of events unfolding one at a time, in just the right time. We took action. A close friend who already lived there invited us for the weekend. We met her real estate agent, researched neighborhoods, and bought an affordable house within a very short period of time. No struggle, no frustration, no resentment.

There's more . . .

We'd moved into our new home, but Derek was still working in New York City with a long commute each morning and night.

He was not able to see our baby when she was awake, and it was wearing him down and making me feel lonely.

We decided to take action and follow the guidance. We asked everyone we knew if they knew someone who worked in fixed income technology at the investment bank down the street. Almost as if on cue, the real estate agent who'd helped us buy the house and had become my new friend said that she actually did know someone in fixed income technology at that particular firm.

We couldn't believe it! After several phone calls, Derek's résumé landed on his future boss's desk. At first the man thought it was a practical joke being played on him. Derek fit the profile he'd been looking for in a candidate to a tee. Within weeks, Derek had been hired. It was better than anything I could have imagined! Everything we had asked for (and more) had been provided to us once we decided to be open and surrender to the guidance.

That said, surrendering is not always an easy thing. For many people who like to have a lot of control in their lives, myself included, it can feel overwhelming to put yourself at the mercy of something intangible. But you can let yourself be guided while still being in control.

Imagine for a moment that you put your hands on a wheel in front of you. This is the wheel of life. Instead of gripping the wheel too tightly, taking sharp turns, and only going where you think you should be going, release the grip just a bit. Keep your hands on the wheel, but let yourself be guided by the wheel itself, knowing that if you really want to, you can take over anytime you want. Let it take you where you are meant to go, without effort on your part.

Just as with this imaginary wheel, when you relinquish the white-knuckled grip on your life, leave behind the arrogance of knowing it all, and let yourself be vulnerable enough to trust that the universe has a plan for you that is more rich than yours, you will achieve even more than you would have on your own.

You are being guided by the universe all day long, every day. Surrender to the guidance, knowing all is well. No more struggling and forcing things to go your way in your life. You will get there with much greater ease and with grace.

48. Once impossible, now easy

"So many of our dreams at first seem
impossible, then they seem improbable, and then,
when we summon the will, they soon become inevitable."

—CHRISTOPHER REEVE

There is a bigger plan for you, bigger than you actually realize or comprehend at this moment. Your potential for achieving greatness is infinitely bigger than you can see right now. You may have heard this before, and you may agree with it intellectually, but perhaps you haven't let it fully sink in. You are the same as God. He made you in His likeness. If this doesn't quite make sense, see if this helps:

Pear trees do not make oranges.

Dogs do not make cats.

The apple doesn't fall far from the tree.

If God is a boundless Creator and you are a child of God, created in His image, what you can create is boundless, as well. If God can play really big, then so can you. You have the capability, the potential, and the wiring to do things in a much bigger way than you are doing them right now.

Because your thoughts create your reality, everything you have in your life is a result of something you've thought about. You can (and do) manifest everything you put your focus on, each and every day. (This is within reason, of course. If you are a woman who is four feet tall, no matter how much you may want to become a six-foot man, the likelihood is slim.)

This means that anything you want to create—a relationship, a certain income, exponential growth in your business, even things that seem impossible and completely out of your reach right now—can and absolutely will be created.

But here's the catch. To manifest and bring into being the thing or circumstance that you would like to experience, you must do two things:

1. Believe that it can actually happen.

2. Expect that it will happen.

This is where a lot of people get sidetracked. Often, especially when people stretch themselves to think much bigger, they don't actually believe it can be done: therefore, they do not expect it to happen. And when you don't believe or expect, you will not attract what you want.

When something feels completely out of reach and impossible, then it will stay impossible. Your mind-set doesn't see how it could ever happen, but remember, feeling that something is impossible only means that you haven't found the solution to achieving it yet. So don't give up.

I'd like to show you a process that I use continually to believe that I can attract and manifest what seems completely and utterly out of my reach. It is a simple process that I call "Once Impossible, Now Easy." Here's how it works:

1. Think of a really big goal, something that you have previously thought you would never be able to achieve, something outside your comfort zone.

2. Ask yourself, "On a scale of 1 to 10, with 1 representing 'I will never be able to achieve that' and 10 representing 'I can totally make that happen,' can I do this?" Check in with your big goal, be honest with yourself, and write down the number that represents your conviction and certainty that you can actually make that happen.

Remember, you cannot attract what you do not believe or expect. So, it's imperative that you have conviction if you want to experience the achievement of that goal. Let's continue. The next few steps are designed to help you strengthen your belief and expectation level.

1. Look back over the course of your life, starting at age four or five and take inventory of your accomplishments.

2. Write down the things you can easily do now that at one point in your life seemed impossible. Start with basic things you take for granted, such as walking, swimming, tying your shoelaces, riding a

bike, receiving an academic achievement, winning a sports competition, driving a car, making a certain amount of money, learning something new, and so on. These are the things that once frightened you that you now consider your "new normal," meaning you can now do them easily and without effort.

The point of this exercise is for you to realize that you've actually achieved and accomplished many things that once seemed difficult. These are things that you never give yourself credit for, but you should. You mastered these tasks. This realization can help give you confidence in your abilities, so you believe that you have what it takes to achieve seemingly impossible things.

It becomes proof that you are indeed more capable than you think.

When I do this exercise for myself, I list all the things from my childhood that we talked about, such as learning how to ride a bike, tying my shoes on my own, and so on. And then I reflect on the following (I share this only to get you thinking about your own list of accomplishments):

- I became fluent in English in a matter of three months when I was ten years old.

- I earned my own money in high school by working in a French pastry shop.

- I moved back to France after leaving college to start my career in Paris with the equivalent of a child's command of the French language.

- I got a job in Paris and wrote for a French marketing magazine at the age of 20.

- I moved to New York City on my own at the age of 21.

- I landed a job in the competitive field of advertising.

- I moved into my own apartment in Manhattan at the age of 22.

- I left my corporate career and became self-employed at the age of 29.

- I met (and married) a wonderful man who loves me.

- I had three beautiful children.

- I created a very successful income.

- I have ten employees and an office overlooking the ocean.

- I have a business that is repeatedly ranked as one of America's fastest-growing companies.

- I went from having a handful of clients a year to hundreds of clients at any given time.

- I moved into my dream house.

- I have built several schools in Kenya and continue to do so.

Keep a long list of these and continually add to it. Alternatively, you can take an index card and write, "Once Impossible, Now Easy: tying my shoe." Whenever you feel overwhelmed by something that seems out of your reach, pull out your list or go through your stack of index cards and allow yourself to feel the confidence growing within you.

Obviously, if you were to show this list to anyone else, it may seem to some people that you were bragging. But that isn't going to happen because this "Once Impossible, Now Easy" list is for your eyes only. It is private and simply meant to have you reflect on your capability in moments when you don't believe in yourself or that something really big could actually happen.

It essentially gives you the self-confidence that then gives you the permission to go for that big goal, even if you didn't believe you can accomplish it at first. It all comes down to what you believe about yourself. Nothing is impossible in the realm of your Creator. If you believe and expect something can happen, even if you have no idea exactly how you'll do it, you will achieve it. That's the way the universe works.

And each time you accomplish something you once thought was impossible and that is now part of your everyday life or skill set, add it to your ever-expanding list. As Anthony Robbins said, "What we can or cannot do, what we consider possible or impossible, is rarely a function of our true capability. It is more likely a function of our beliefs about who we are."

This process is about getting confidence from your past achievements. It allows you to move past the fear of not feeling good enough and into the realm of the possible. It turns what you are afraid of from Mission Impossible to Mission Possible, turning what seems insurmountable into the new normal.

And that is how you can accomplish anything you set your mind to. The evidence of your past capabilities helps you believe and expect a positive outcome. That's when the universe gives you what you want.

49. The vortex of creation

"When you are in a state of allowing, which means you have quieted your mind—or focused your mind in such a way that there is an absence, or a decreasing, of resistant thought—your Vibration naturally rises . . . and when your natural Vibration rises, you will have achieved a different and improved point of attraction . . . and your life just gets better and better."

—ABRAHAM HICKS

Some people have the ability to create a rich, meaningful, abundant life they love, while others continually struggle and get in their own way. Through the years I have learned that where a person lands on this is not so much based on their life circumstances but, rather, on how they view themselves and how they feel about their lives.

Although many see their current life situations as being a direct result of the "cards they were dealt" in life—such as being born in poverty; having critical, unsupportive parents; coming from a disadvantaged background; or having endured difficult, even painful life experiences—there are countless examples of people who have transcended their circumstances to create extraordinary results, against all odds.

I believe that each one of us creates our life based on what we believe and how we feel, that our mind-set creates our reality. If we come from a mind-set that is based on feelings of lack (that there is limited wealth, that life is hard and unfair, that things are getting worse instead of better), then we will create lack. Conversely, if we approach the game of life using an abundance perspective (where there is plenty for everyone, that things are getting better, and opportunities abound), then we experience abundance in our results, in money, meaning, and happiness. Here's what I mean:

I've discovered four different scenarios in people's mind-sets about creating abundance. Their level of manifestation is directly correlated to the balance of two factors: (1) how big their future vision is, and (2) their current level of contentment with their current situation. Here's how it plays out:

1. If you are feeling resentful, angry, and disappointed about what you have now *and* you don't have a big vision or big goals, you are likely to feel negative about your prospects for your future. *This is a mind-set based in lack.*

2. If you are someone who is happy *but* doesn't think bigger about what's possible for you, then you will likely not take any big leaps, which means you will probably stay in your

current situation, without advancing much. You'll continue to be content, but you won't accomplish anything much bigger. *This is a "playing small" mind-set.*

3. If you are someone who has big goals and understands that there is a bigger future for you, *but* you're impatient, frustrated, and focused on the fact that things aren't moving quickly enough, and you believe that you'll only be happy when you achieve a particular thing, you will likely not advance very quickly as you are also focused in lack. *This is a mind-set based in frustration and stress.*

4. If you are someone who is happy with your life, feeling grateful and blessed for what you do have and what you've already accomplished *and* you have a big, positive vision for your future, and you know that your happiness is not tied to you achieving that big vision, then you will continually create more of what you want in your life and achieve results that astound others around you. *This is a mind-set based in abundance.*

You see, how you feel and what you believe about your potential actually dictate what opportunities you attract and whether or not you take action on the opportunities that show up. If you are angry, feel deprived and resentful, and believe that nothing good ever happens, then you will likely not act on opportunities that come your way. A mind-set of lack begets more lack.

Conversely, if you come from a mind-set of abundance and positive expectation, feeling happy, content, pleasantly optimistic, knowing that you are being guided and always expecting that good things will come to you, you will see an opportunity as your pathway to creating the future you have dreamed of. Then you will act on that opportunity. Abundance thinking begets more abundance.

I noticed this with my students over the years. The ones who felt happy about their current accomplishments and were positive about their futures would always take more action on the assignments I gave them. They had more confidence and were more courageous when presented with a challenge to play a bigger game. At the same time, those who were resentful, angry that their results weren't happening fast enough, and quick to blame outside circumstances—and who continually compared themselves with more successful people— were often stuck in a holding pattern and rarely accomplished their goals.

The good news is that how you feel and how big you decide to play is a choice. You have the ability to change your mind-set and, therefore, your results. I know this because I have belonged, at one time or another, in each of the four mind-set categories I listed above. Early on in my career, when I was working a corporate job, I distinctly remember opening up my paycheck to see a very small dollar amount, despite all the late hours I put in just to get my work done. Tears welled up in my eyes that day, and I felt hopeless and helpless, and I didn't see much of a future for myself. *(I wasn't happy, nor did I have a big vision for my future.)*

Then there was a period when I started doing personal growth and development work to clean up my mind-set, and I was happier, but I was content with reaching very small goals, only increasing my results in teeny, tiny incremental ways. *(I was happier but had no big vision, so I was playing small in my life.)*

I have also been in a place where I had big goals for myself and, based on my increasing results, I believed that I had it within me to achieve more, but I constantly compared myself with others in my field who were advancing faster than I was, making more money than I was. Although I publicly applauded them for their success, in my own thoughts, I resented them and sometimes felt rage when thinking of how easy their success seemed, while I was frustrated about my lack of advancement. *(I had a big vision, but I wasn't happy at all.)*

And, finally, I've arrived at a point in my life where I'm happy and grateful for who I've become, all the work I've put in, and what I've accomplished. Even in the midst of life's challenges, I realize that things could be much worse. I reach for bigger results because I know I'm capable of accomplishing more, and yet my happiness is not tied to this next level. *(This is when you enter the vortex of manifestation, an abundance state of mind, and precisely when you start creating a life you love.)*

Now, I understand that some might say, "Well, it's easy to feel abundant when you're successful. You have less to worry about." But here's what I've discovered: when you act from an abundance mind-set, the abundance shows up. Not before. *The mind-set precedes the results, always.*

I noticed that when my students were *simultaneously* happy *and* positively expecting great results, they would achieve those results. When they felt good about life, good things would happen to them.

For years, I used to joke about the "Client Attraction Vortex" that my students and I would create when we all came together for our group mastermind meetings. At these meetings, we would celebrate each other's successes, dream bigger dreams for their businesses, strategize together, support each other unconditionally, have a great time (sometimes even dance!), build momentum, increase their self-confidence, solve their challenges, and champion each other's accomplishments without judgment or resentment. We were feeling really good.

And at the very same time my students would report amazing things happening in their businesses, such as new opportunities presenting themselves, unexpected money materializing, prospects contacting them wanting to become clients . . . all during our meetings. At first, I thought it was a coincidence.

Not anymore! It became clear that when they felt good, they got more clients and made more money. When they felt positive and confident, they implemented more, took bigger chances, and increased their results. When they focused on their big visions and next steps while happy, the results came quickly. It almost became predictable.

Conversely, I also realized that if they worked on their marketing while in a place of resentment for a lack of results, they wouldn't get clients and would continue to struggle. No matter how hard they worked, if they didn't feel good at the time they were implementing their assignments, they wouldn't create positive results.

Years later, I learned that there actually *is* such a thing as a vortex of manifestation. It depends on how you *feel* in the moment you are thinking about creating your bigger future. If you want to create positive results in your life, then you must be in a "feeling good" place first. Get into the vortex (be grateful about your life as it is now) and *then* create your vision for this bigger future. Be happy about what you've created so far, and once you're in that happy state of mind, *then and only then* take the steps necessary to achieve that future.

If your energy is rooted in lack, then don't bother taking big action on your goals. Wait until you get in a happier, more grateful state of mind. Now, as anyone will tell you, this is simple but not always easy. When you're feeling hopeless and helpless, it can be really difficult to change your outlook on life, especially when the bills are piled high on your desk and the number in your bank account is very low. (I remember this all too well.)

Getting into the vortex is simply a matter of changing your emotional state of mind while increasing your personal vibration from a lower level to a higher level. If you find yourself in a state of mind that is resentful, where you feel hopeless, or where you feel you are putting in a lot of effort with few results, here are a few simple ways of getting back into that vortex of manifestation:

- Make a list of things you absolutely love to do and that make you feel really good (reading, walking on the beach with your dog, playing with your cat, arranging flowers, volunteering at a soup kitchen, and so on) and then do one of them.

- Meditate.

- Dance to your favorite music, especially if no one's watching (my favorite).

- Do yoga.

- Watch one of your favorite movies, making sure that it's a happy, funny, or inspirational film.

- Spend time in nature.

- Take a calming aromatherapy bath.

- Take a nap.

The idea is to change how you feel in that moment . . . and then, once you feel good and optimistic again, go back to dreaming bigger and doing what it takes to create results.

That's when you set yourself up for positively changing your results and allow yourself to play a much bigger game, no matter what your current reality says.

50. This is how you do it

"There's always a way if you're committed."

—ANTHONY ROBBINS

Whenever you have an idea, there is a way to do it, even when you don't know how you will ever accomplish it. Just the fact that you had the idea in the first place means that it can be done. If you are able to dream it, then there is a way to get it. That's when the universe steps in—but not before you make a decision to have it or achieve it.

Most people stop themselves from wanting something (especially something that feels way out of their comfort zones) because they don't see how they could ever get it or achieve it. But if you understand the process for manifesting what you want in any aspect of your life, you will be able to achieve it.

The key is to make a decision first about what you want. Without the initial decision and commitment to that vision, it's just a hope. A declaration is what the universe responds to.

The way the universe works to give you what you want is to first require that you make a firm decision that you want it and will get it. Have conviction. You must have a clear picture in your mind about what you want, the end result, and make a commitment as well as a declaration that you will get it. That's when you will be shown the way to get it. You don't need to know how it will happen, because that's not your job. That's the universe's job.

Instead of making the decision and commitment first, most people wait for opportunities to show up before they will commit. They wait for the detailed plan about how it will happen before they say, "Yes, I want that."

But the universe doesn't respond to that. It responds to your conviction and your belief that what you want is on its way to you already, without you having it all figured out ahead of time. You don't need to see the whole picture that's ahead, just the next couple of steps you need to take.

When you zero in on what you want and decide that it will be yours, then the way to get it done will come to you in the form of opportunities, signs, and guidance about what to do next. You just have to be patient.

How do you make a decision? Think of what you really want in your life and write it down. Remove all limitations and belief that you can't have it and stay with the belief that it can be done.

You must first ask for the thing you want. The universe, although it is aware of what's going on in your life, cannot deliver something to you unless you ask first. Be clear about what you want to accomplish or receive.

For many people, the idea of getting clear on what they want is a task in itself. This happened to me years ago. I was so accustomed to feeling like I didn't deserve the best in life that I was disconnected from what I really wanted. So I made a list of what I didn't like or what I didn't want to have in my life, things that were currently in my life, and things I never wanted to experience. When I finished with this list, I flipped every item from a negative to a positive. If I had written, "I never want to be landlocked," then I flipped it to, "I love living by the beach." If I had written, "I don't want to be in debt," I flipped it to, "I always have plenty of money for anything I'd like to buy," and so on.

In fact, almost everything I have in my life now is something I've asked for, from my husband (I made a detailed list of the kind of person I wanted to attract and be with), to my children, my business, my income, my home, and so on. I did this even though I didn't consciously know what the next steps were going to be or how the goal would ever happen. But I was clear on the end result, and I stayed focused on that end result, no matter what distractions or obstacles got in the way. I held on to that vision no matter what I saw in front of me. And because of that, the vision happened.

Next, it's time to get out of the way. Stop trying to control how it will happen, who will help you, or when it should happen. Let the universe be in charge of that. The whole process will be easier and happen much faster than if you try to force the process yourself. Remember, you control the end result, but the process of how it will happen is not your job.

Finally, be still and open to the guidance we've been talking about. There will be signs and happy coincidences, and you must follow them. Do not take them for granted. You will know when it's a sign because it'll be something so out of the blue, so unexpected, and so exactly what you asked for that you'll realize there is a greater force at work. You will know intuitively that what you are experiencing is a sign.

In fact, I once asked the universe for something very specific—a solution to a problem with someone stealing my intellectual property and passing it off as her own. As I was making this request in my journal, I added one last sentence. It went something like, "Please give me guidance on how to accomplish this. Let the clue be so out of the ordinary, so unusual, that I will know it's coming from you and only you." And it did. I was guided to take a look back at my e-mail order receipts and there I found proof that this person had indeed purchased my proprietary system. I smiled and actually got a little teary, knowing that the universe rearranged itself to fulfill my wish. As a result, this person's attorney fired her and she immediately stopped what she was doing.

I still am moved whenever this happens. It is very humbling for me to know that I have so much power to create my life, as you do.

Here's a recap:

1. Ask.
2. Stay focused on the end result.
3. Believe that it's on its way to you, no matter what you see in front of you.
4. Watch for the signs.
5. Take action on the signs.
6. Be grateful.

51. The signs are everywhere

"There is no such thing as chance; and what to us seems merest accident springs from the deepest source of destiny."

—FRIEDRICH SCHILLER

Remember, you are never presented with an opportunity without also being given the way to accomplish it. The universe wants to see you reach your goals. It is ready to put your plan in motion at the first sign of your decision and conviction. Everything you need—money, the right people, the resources, and the skills—will be given to you just when you need it.

If you've asked, the guidance will be given to you on the inside, in the form of hunches, gut feelings, and intuitive "downloads." On the outside, guidance will come in the form of signs, coincidences, people coming into your life at the perfect time, and things landing in your lap unexpectedly. This is your step-by-step plan to accomplish what you want, and it is only given to you little by little.

For me, I get a word or hear a song on the radio with lyrics that are the answer to what I've been looking for. (Even if I've known the song for 15 years, the words will seem like they are new to me.) Repetition is a clear sign. For example, I repeatedly heard that I should read a particular book. I ordered it online but put it on the shelf without reading it. A couple of months later, I received the very same book again, even though I had not ordered another copy nor had anyone give it to me. Seeing the repetition, I immediately read the book, which gave me the answer to what I had been asking.

Sometimes these signs are obvious, like receiving a book twice, and sometimes they are very subtle. That's why you've got to practice listening and paying attention to the guidance. I recommend writing anything that comes up in a small notebook that you carry around with you at all times. Take notes when signs and nudges show up. They are like the bread crumbs that are laid in your path to guide you to the next step.

All you have to do is pay attention. Stay focused on finding the signs. When you receive them, pay attention and take action. That's all you have to do.

52. The day you plant the seed . . .

> *"I am extraordinarily patient,*
> *provided I get my own way in the end."*
>
> —MARGARET THATCHER

It sometimes takes time for the universe to rearrange itself to accommodate your request. The day you plant the seed is not the day you eat the fruit. Sometimes people get frustrated and impatient when they see that what they've asked for isn't here yet. They give up on believing that it's on its way.

We've been raised with so many instant-gratification claims swirling around us—"Thinner thighs in 30 days," "Quit smoking in one session," or "Make a million dollars in a week"—that it's easy to expect things to miraculously happen in a very short period of time. The problem is that's not necessarily on the universe's timeline.

Yes, I admit that many extraordinary things can be accomplished quickly under extreme circumstances or with a lot of experience. But for most people, thinking like this can set up unrealistic expectations of what's to come, and when our initial efforts don't meet those grandiose expectations quickly, frustration sets in.

When there's a delay in seeing results from an action you've taken, here's the process that sometimes follows:

1. Doubt creeps in

2. Then worry

3. Followed by fear

4. Frustration and irrational anger (at yourself, at others, at anything)

5. Resentment and bitterness

6. Giving up

This is where many people throw out the baby with the bathwater and completely give up on their dreams.

Sometimes when you try something new, you'll see results immediately, which is comforting. But then, as you begin to stretch beyond your comfort zone and go after bigger dreams that require even more effort, sometimes the results need time to take root. That's when you may scratch your head and say, "Where are all the results? I mean, I've been working my butt off over here! Where are the millions of dollars? I expected to see results!"

It's not easy to be patient, and it's probably harder now than ever before, especially when information can be sent across the world in a nanosecond and with the microchip's capacity multiplying every few months.

In all things, there is a gestation period. Think of pregnancy. There's a reason that it takes nine months for a baby to be born at full term. It simply takes that long for the gestation process to occur. You wouldn't want to rush the process and have the baby arrive any sooner than it's supposed to. With pregnancy, we accept that it will take that long for the baby to mature. Instead of getting frustrated and angry, we take our time picking out paint colors for the nursery, researching the meaning of names, and getting ready for this new little life to join ours. We are patient, even if in the last few weeks we grow impatient as we become more uncomfortable. We honor the process of gestation.

And yet with other things in life, we do not always honor the gestation period that's required for the universe to rearrange itself for the outcome we've asked for. But it's absolutely necessary. Yes, miracles can happen (and do happen) in short periods of time. But the really important stuff can take a while. Sometimes even a long time, much longer than you think it would or should.

Every arduous journey has begun by taking that initial step. Every other step you take builds on that first one. It's a process, not an event, and life is about progress, not perfection. Pace, not race. The more you keep taking steps toward what you want, the closer you get. It might not show up according to your desired timeline, but when you point your feet in the right direction and take step after step, you are getting closer to what you want each minute. When you see a glimpse of progress, celebrate it, even if you're not quite there yet.

Sometimes you'll take a step back. You might even take many steps back. But don't be hard on yourself. There is no straight line in the universe. Even when you set your sights on a target, you will veer off at some point. Yes, you have plans and your own timeline, but things don't always work out as planned. Choose to gracefully accept the twists and turns, and then veer back toward your target.

Here's the thing you must remember: almost anything really good in life will require time and dedication to become a reality. If you become impatient with the process, you're more likely to give up on relationships, goals, and other things that are important to you.

It takes time for the seeds you've planted to put down roots, sprout, grow, and then bear fruit that you can eat. That's why you have to be diligent about planting them quickly and doing whatever it takes to foster them. At the same time, it's important to plant as many seeds as possible so that you have different things cropping up. Don't rely on just one thing to create results.

Instead of being in a place of resentment (which will never quickly attract what you want), remember to keep yourself in a place of positive expectation. There is a sign that I made for my office and I have been referring to it on a daily basis for many, many years: I am positively expecting great results, no matter what I see in front of me. The universe is rearranging itself for my best interest right now.

I've given it to my employees, students, private clients, spouse, children, friends, and everyone who needs to stay in positive expectation.

Your voice is being heard. Be patient; it's on its way. Be in a place of quiet assurance that what you want is getting ready to be sent to you. Once your decision is made, your only job is to be committed to the vision, believe, and follow the guidance.

In fact, this is something I add at the end of any request I make. "I release this intention to you, universe, knowing it is fulfilled with grace and beauty each moment. I know that it is already on its way to me. And so it is."

This mantra has gotten me through countless bouts of impatience. If ever I get caught up in thinking, *Why isn't this happening fast enough?* getting into a place of self-doubt, or blaming the process, I remind myself of this, and things seem to just work themselves out rather quickly. That's when a sign shows up, the project advances, and the results start coming in. But if I stay in that place of doubt, worry, or, worse, blame, it surely gets worse.

You are ultimately responsible for your own successes, your actions, and, most important, how you see your own progress. You create your future and your results based on how you choose to see the world and the way you react to life. A person coming from a victim's point of view will always see fault in the process. That's universal law. A person coming from a victorious point of view will always see opportunity, no matter what's in front of them.

You've got to have patience and perseverance. Just as you wouldn't rush Mother Nature and expect a tree to grow in one day, blaming the process of the universe for being too slow doesn't work. Tend to your seeds. Do everything that's required of you. Understand that different plants sprout at different paces, and then get yourself in a place of positive expectation. Don't worry. Don't get frustrated. Be persistent. Believe that what you want is on its way to you.

Miraculously, that's when the results happen, quicker than you thought possible.

53. You've got a lot of rules!

> *"Hell, there are no rules here—we're trying to accomplish something."*
>
> —THOMAS A. EDISON

The funny thing about manifesting is that what you want will not always come from the source you expect. Sometimes we put parameters around where we think the something will come from, and we only focus on looking for the opportunities there, turning a blind eye to other sources.

I once had a client who set as a goal that she wanted to make a sizable amount of money in her business within that year. She was determined to sign up enough clients in one year to bring in $250,000 in revenues. When that exact amount came in through her real estate investment properties instead of her business, she was deeply disappointed in herself and upset with the manifesting process. She felt like she'd failed.

Her mastermind colleagues tried to reassure her again and again that she did indeed manifest the money, but that it hadn't shown up exactly the way she'd expected it. She hadn't realized that she'd had a rigid rule around where the money was going to come from, but that in the end, the result was the same.

Years ago, I set an intention to manifest a car that I could afford on my limited income. I was living by myself in New York City at the time, and I yearned to go away on weekends, to get out of the city without taking public transportation. I had no idea how I would afford a new car, but I set my intention and then surrendered it to the universe.

Nothing happened for a while, and then it all happened one night. During one of monthly dinners I shared with my stepfather, out of the blue, he asked me if any of my friends would like to buy my stepbrother's old college car for a few hundred dollars. I nearly fell off my chair. I said, "Oh, I've been wanting to buy a car. I had no idea John was selling his. I'll buy it!" My stepfather hadn't known I was in the market for a car, and I didn't know he was in the market to sell a car. When I set the intention, it came from the unlikeliest of places. And affordable it was! I ended up driving that car for many years, until our first child was born.

Beware of the rules you have around what you want to manifest in your life.

Sometimes your biggest opportunity will come from an apparent misfortune, like losing a job. When I was a secretary working in a Manhattan advertising agency, one of my colleagues, also a secretary, got laid off. At first, she was terrified of not finding another job. But when I bumped into her a few months later, she was beaming from ear to ear. She had used the opportunity of getting laid off to start her own business creating beautiful dresses out of African textiles. It was her passion, and she was very successful at it.

Remember that there's a reason for everything. What you most want (or need) will sometimes come from an unexpected source. Be grateful for it.

Chapter 9

Trust Your Intuition

54. It's always there if you listen

*"Every time you don't follow your inner
guidance, you feel a loss of energy, loss of power,
a sense of spiritual or emotional deadness."*

—SHAKTI GAWAIN

Intuition is difficult to explain. We refer to it as a hunch, a gut feeling, an instinct, a knowing, an inner guidance, or just a feeling that we use to make decisions and take action. It's like a quiet flash of information, giving you what you need, when you need it most, to get what you want.

Intuition is all of those things, and it is also spirit, guiding you through your instincts and the sum of your experiences. This guidance doesn't come from just you or your brain. Your higher self is feeding you the guidance.

Intuition is always there, with you at all times. It is always available and we all have it, although some people have developed it more than others. You can develop it more at any time you choose. It's there to help you in your decisions and your judgments. Even if you don't believe it at first because you don't see it, all you need to do to have access to it is realize that it's always at your fingertips, whenever you look for it.

The key to using your intuition is not to force it. You must become very aware of the subtle direction you are being given. These are whispers at most . . . a feeling inside, a hunch to take a different route or to call a friend, to buy a particular book or to leave a restaurant. It's better to just let it happen naturally and trust something within yourself to guide you. It's about being an open vessel for guidance and paying attention. It's there if you make yourself available to get advice from your source.

I'm continually working on sharpening my intuition. It's simple, and you can use it anytime and anywhere. In fact, some of the tasks that made me realize I had access to my intuition are pretty mundane, but over and over again, these have proved to me that when I don't listen to that little inner voice, I make mistakes.

Listening to your intuition can be as simple as getting a hunch to reduce the amount of salt when you're cooking—ignore this, and the dish ends up too salty. Or you ignore the gut feeling that you shouldn't buy that pair of peach shoes, even though they are on sale—and then you never wear them even once.

Your intuition can give you the answer you've been looking for. One day as I was setting up my own business,

I was looking for some file cabinets online. Money was tight, so I wanted a bargain on a tall three-drawer file cabinet. The price on the ones I found online at the office supplier seemed astronomical, and after looking for close to an hour, I gave up.

On my way out, I got the feeling that I should take a different route home. It didn't make sense to me because the route was slightly longer, but I decided to go ahead and follow the guidance. Just as I was getting close to home, I rounded the corner on this route I would never have taken, and there, right on the sidewalk, were dozens of used three-drawer file cabinets. My jaw dropped. The office a block away from my home was liquidating all its office furniture, and the file cabinets were on sale for five dollars. I bought one on the spot, looked up at the sky, shook my head, and smiled, saying, "Thank you."

There are times when you realize that your life wouldn't have been the same if you'd chosen to ignore a gut feeling. This is what happened to me when I was in college. My mother and I hadn't talked in several weeks, as I'd been upset with her. One afternoon, I got the strongest urge to call her. I picked up the phone, even though part of me thought this didn't make sense, and ended up having the most wonderful, loving, hour-long conversation with her, the most we'd ever talked. I will never forget this because it's the last time I spoke to her. Hours later, she died in a fatal car accident.

This was one of the first times I really paid attention to how important it is to listen to your intuition. Had I not listened to that very strong gut feeling, I would never have forgiven myself for not having called her. It stunned me and made me realize that there was something bigger than me guiding my life. This was also the very first time I truly believed there was a higher power, that God wasn't just an idea. It now felt real for me.

You can use your intuition in your everyday life, when you're stuck and don't know what to say next or do next. The next step or word is given to you if you tune in and become a vessel for guidance. I do this onstage when speaking to large audiences, with my students and clients, on phone consultations, and when writing marketing copy or books. If I'm not sure what to say out loud, I quietly say to myself, "Universe, please help me here. Please send me some guidance." Then I usually get a word, an image, or a knowing of what to say next. It's miraculous how dependable it can be the more you practice it. I never have to worry about what to say next. I'm supported the whole time, and you can be, too.

The idea is that you must trust yourself with this. The more you act on that voice, that image, that feeling, or that knowing, the more signs you receive. The best way to increase your intuitive capabilities is by tapping into them often. We all receive intuitive guidance; it just depends on how willing you are to notice it and trust it, knowing it is here to support you. Practice it often, and at first with little things. The more you see it working, the more you can move up to bigger and bigger things.

55. Everyone's different

"Now I realize after all these years in my career, that guidance comes to different people in different ways! Some people obtain it just through quiet meditation and Bible reading, to others divine guidance arrives at odd moments in the form of quiet mental nudgings from God and His Spirit."

—VIRGINIA BRANDT BERG

Guidance comes in different ways. People see quick flashes of images, hear a subtle voice or word, get a physical feeling, or have a knowing about something. Determine what kind of spiritual guidance you tend to get most often by assessing which senses you connect to most.

There are five intuitive senses: clairvoyance (clear seeing), clairaudience (clear hearing), claircognizance (clear knowing), clairsentience (clear feeling), and clair-gustience (clear smell/taste). Most people have access to all five intuitive capabilities and are particularly strong at two or three of them.

For me, words get fed to me when I'm writing and when I'm speaking to people. The next right word will show up, and I've practiced this enough to realize that it's being fed to me; it's not coming from me. Usually this happens just one word at a time.

I have also noticed that when something is particularly true or the universe wants to confirm the validity of something I'm saying or that's being said to me, I will get immediate chills up and down my arms and legs or my entire body. Sometimes I will be moved to tears (clear feeling). I also get a knowing once in a while and sometimes get an image fed to me, but these aren't as common as the other two forms of guidance.

Once I got clear on which of the five senses I am most connected to, it allowed me to focus much more on the guidance. I recommend you do the same. Ask for guidance and see how it shows up most often. You can practice this on your own. The more you do, the easier it will become. You will get a much clearer insight as to how you receive intuitive information.

56. Declutter to better decipher

"For everyone who asks receives."

—Luke 11:10

You always have a guide on your shoulder, leading you down the right path. If things aren't going as well for you as you'd like, it probably means you're not listening to your intuition or not taking action on the guidance that you're receiving. Something's getting in the way.

- Are you actually listening?

- Are you being arrogant or a know-it-all?

- Are you keeping too busy?

- Are you numbing out on sugar, processed food, work, alcohol, or drugs?

- Are you second-guessing yourself?

If you're having a difficult time listening to your intuition, you must slow down and declutter your mind to decipher the guidance.

This may mean that you take out a journal and do a "brain drain." Just write and write and write anything that comes into your mind without stopping. Even if it's nonsensical, even if you write, "I don't know what to write," just empty your mind. This is not about correctness but rather about dumping what's in your head onto paper.

Clarity in your mind will give you clarity in your intuition. Sometimes it's the physical space around you that must be cleared.

Clutter in your immediate physical space creates clutter in your mind. Before writing any sizable book or marketing copy, I find myself obsessively tidying my desk and clearing my physical space.

When I do, I feel the intuitive guidance more clearly, helping me remember to put things in my writing that I would have forgotten otherwise. I seem to write better.

Reduce or put a pause on consuming substances that cause you to numb out or on doing activities that cloud your thinking. When I'm focusing on a big project, I clean up my food. I eat less sugar, flour, cheese, processed food, and meat, and drink less wine. Those things cause me to be more scattered. Virtually every time I do this, the guidance becomes easier to decipher.

Shift into the creative side of your brain and do some creative or relaxing activities, versus focusing on analytical stuff. Divine guidance can be better heard when you are in silence or in a meditative state, even if you don't meditate. Go for a long walk, sit by the ocean, garden, pet an animal, dance, write in a journal, ski, run outdoors, listen to music, paint, or cook for pleasure . . . anything that calms your mind and helps you get out of your head.

When you do this, you increase your ability to receive guidance from the universe. The idea is to quiet the chatter and repetitive thoughts in your mind, letting go of your worries so you can create a clear vessel for the intuition to come through. Find some sort of meditative practice you are comfortable with that takes you into the present moment and do that practice more often. You will then get the guidance loud and clear.

57. Intuition or inner gremlin?

"If you hear a voice within you say 'you cannot paint,' then by all means paint, and that voice will be silenced."

—VINCENT VAN GOGH

People often ask me how to determine what's intuition and what's that other voice we hear inside. Having two voices going on in your head at the same time, saying things that are the opposite of your conscious voice, feels like a tug-of-war. It's difficult to decipher which voice you should listen to. One is based on love, the other on fear. One wants the best for you; the other wants to take you down. Which voice you listen to determines whether you create a good life or a life of struggle.

The inner gremlin, which I sometimes also refer to as the inner critic or the drunk monkey in your head, is the inner voice that makes you question yourself. It makes you doubt your abilities and gets you thinking that you're not good enough. It is negative, scolding, and aggressive, and it always steers you away from what you want, thwarting your best-laid plans. It is mean and chips away at your self-confidence. It calls you stupid. It suggests you have another piece of cake when you're trying to lose weight. It rationalizes doing something you know you shouldn't be doing. It's the voice inside that tells you that you don't have what it takes to succeed and that you might as well just stop trying. It is loud, defeating, and repetitive. It is the fear-based ego trying to keep you small. It does not love you.

Sadly, this is the voice that most people listen to and take advice from.

The other voice you hear inside loves you. It wants the best for you. It leads you lovingly toward the next thing you should do for your best life. It is always positive and caring. It is soft, subtle, and gentle. It gives you confidence, is trusting, and makes you feel safe. It is your intuition. It is God whispering guidance and love to you, telling you that you are magnificent, that you can accomplish anything.

This voice believes in you. It is telling you that it is ready to help you get what is in your best interest. It is a very faint voice, much more difficult to distinguish than the other. That's why most people don't hear it under the loud, repetitive scolding of the inner gremlin.

Which voice you listen to and take advice from creates your life. The more you listen to the inner gremlin telling you to play small and stay safe, the more you let it take your motivation and chip away at your confidence, the more you will create a life of struggle.

The more you listen to your intuition and the loving voice of your Creator, gently guiding you to make the best decisions, the more you will feel supported and loved, and the more likely you are to create a truly magnificent life. When you choose to ignore the inner critic and instead take advice from the loving voice of intuition, you can turn your life around instantly.

Chapter 10

Go Beyond Fear and Resistance

58. Fear and the beige existence

"When man's mind is confused by fear,
he is in no condition to accept an opportunity."

—RAYMOND HOLLIWELL

To live a richer, more abundant life, you must be willing to not settle for what's convenient and instead be willing to go for what you really want in life, especially if it's out of your current comfort zone. Too many people live a mediocre existence, just getting through the day, not loving their lives because they don't reach for something bigger than what's immediately in front of them.

The biggest obstacle to you living your best life of meaning, purpose, fulfillment, and abundance is the idea that you don't deserve to live it, that you're not good enough to have it. Because of that, you keep yourself small. The fear of what will happen if you begin to change your situation stands in your way. Many people live a beige existence because of fear. Because the fear is so consuming, they stay exactly where they are now, not reaching for the thing they deeply want to experience or accomplish.

Fear will always show up when you reach for a fuller, richer life. Here are examples of fears that come up when you begin thinking about improving your life by reaching for something outside your comfort zone:

Fear of rejection

Fear of being overwhelmed

Fear of success

Fear of failure

Fear of what others will think of you

Fear of humiliation

Fear of making mistakes

Fear of becoming greedy

Fear of change

Fear of the unknown

Fear of confrontation

Fear of losing your freedom

Fear of what others will think if you succeed

Fear of facing your deepest truth

Fear of criticism

Fear that it won't work

Fear of your own power

Fear of losing love

Fear of growing too big

Fear of losing it all

Fear of being exposed

Fear of not being able to pay the bills

Fear of not being good enough

Fear of not doing things right

Fear of being vulnerable

Fear of being fully authentic

Fear of getting hurt

Fear of poverty

Fear of not fitting in

Fear of not having enough

Fear of disapproval

Which of these fears have you felt? How have they stopped you from taking action on opportunities you asked for?

Any one of these will stop most people in their tracks. The problem is that there are usually several fears that come up at the same time. When they do, the first thing we do is retreat, abandoning what we were going after and staying small. Then we rationalize giving up on our dreams by remembering the phrase that was drilled into our consciousness during our childhood: "A bird in the hand is worth two in the bush!" We ask ourselves, "Who do I think I am, anyway? Who am I to want this much? Why can't I just be happy with what I already have?"

That's where it all falls apart. The nail gets pounded into the coffin of your big dreams, the ones that will never materialize.

If you'd like a copy of the list of fears I've identified, you can download one from www.EmbraceYour Magnificence.com/resources.

59. The ego's wrath

*"The Opponent . . . He is the unseen cause of chaos
in the physical world and in the human spirit. His is the
voice that whispers, 'Eat the cake now. Start the diet again on
Monday.' It is he who arouses feelings of despair, pessimism,
fear, anxiety, doubt, and uncertainty."*

—YEHUDA BERG

Where does fear come from, anyway?

To understand why there is struggle in your world or why you are stuck in a rut, you must understand that you have an insidious opponent in this game of life: the ego. The ego is what makes you question yourself and doubt your abilities. It also makes you feel insecure and messes up your best intentions. It is the fear-based inner gremlin urging you to give up when you try something new, such as exercising, writing a book, discarding a bad habit, or reaching for that next level. The more it keeps you small and stuck, the longer it survives.

Although you cannot see the ego, it is your ruthless adversary in everything you do to better your life. One of its many advantages is that it lives within you, in the human mind, but its voice sounds like your voice. It is an aspect of yourself that is hidden. Because it is barely perceptible to most people, it runs the show, controlling a large percentage of your actions and decisions.

The ego is selfish, consistently focused on preserving itself and the status quo. It abhors change and will fight like hell to keep you small. The bigger you decide to play in your life and the more important the dream, goal, or vision you have, the more you enrage the ego and the more resistance you will encounter as you pursue that goal.

When you attempt to stretch beyond your comfort zone, the ego senses it is losing its power over you and feels threatened, fearing its own demise. To protect itself against change, it wages a war for survival against your plans for growth. It creates obstacles to prevent you from advancing. It unleashes your inner gremlin, your negative self-talk—anything that will push you back into the status quo.

"Who do you think you are, anyway?"

"This isn't for you. You can't do this!"

"You don't really deserve success."

"You're not good enough to succeed."

"You've tried this before. It didn't work then, and it won't work now."

"It's going to be too hard and take too long. Just give up now."

"You're so stupid! You'll never amount to anything, so why bother?"

I believe that if we talked to children the way the ego talks to us when it feels threatened, people would call social services on us. That's how brutal the language can be. But understand that this dialogue is not real. It's just the ego creating doubt because it's scared of your growth.

That's the negative self-talk. Now let's get to the ego's greatest weapon against you: fear.

Under the guise of keeping you safe from harm, the ego fills you with fear to stop you. It counsels you to retreat back to "safety." It invokes fear of failure, fear of rejection, fear of criticism, fear of abandonment, and fear of loss of love. Fear is one of the most destructive, paralyzing factors that keep you from playing a bigger game. Fear is the ego's greatest and most effective weapon against you—because, sadly, it works.

This is the ego's wrath, and you should be prepared for it. It's not just one fear, it's everything at once, and it can be very effective at keeping you small. At this panic point, most people retreat to the safety of what they know. I refer to it as "the big breakdown before the big breakthrough."

The more you reach, the more the ego unleashes its weapons of fear. This is why most people never reach their potential or accomplish what they set out to do, because the fear can seem so debilitating. Fear feels uncomfortable, and most people avoid discomfort like the plague.

If you want to get to that next level, whatever that is for you, you simply must be willing to stretch beyond your existing comfort zone. It requires being comfortable with being uncomfortable, at least for a short time. You feel the fear but take action anyway.

What you want (the breakthrough) is right beyond the panic point. Like labor pains, it's excruciating but short-lived, and what you get on the other side is the greatest abundance and joy. Yes, it's scary at first. But it won't kill you. Remember that fear is just a trick being played on you by the ego.

Be courageous. Don't allow the fear to consume you. Stay focused on your outcome. The more action you take toward your goal, in spite of the negative talk, fear, worry, and doubt, the faster the ego lessens its grip on you. Eventually ego retreats and you get the breakthrough you've been looking for.

The discomfort is always strongest the first time or when you are playing your biggest game yet. But once you recognize ego's ways, you realize this is a game you want to play because the rewards of crossing the panic point are so worthwhile. Once accustomed to this dance (or war) with your ego, you will recognize it and say, "Oh, I must be on the verge of a big breakthrough! Cool! Bring it on . . ."

It helps to surround yourself with people who have successfully crossed the panic point many times. They can coach you through it and reassure you that you're on the right track. This willingness to stay the course is what separates people who live full, rich, and abundant lives from those who live a beige existence.

This is a rite of passage for all who play bigger.

60. The only reality

"The fear is not real, Dil Bahadur; it is only in your mind, like all other things. Our thoughts form what we believe to be reality."

—ISABEL ALLENDE

Although your fears feel real, they don't actually exist. Here's why. The experience of fear is an attempt to avoid perceived future pain—the anticipation of what might happen that hasn't happened yet and most likely will not happen. The thing you are afraid of is not likely or guaranteed, but the fear you feel makes it appear real and imminent.

Because what you fear hasn't happened yet, it is a projection into the future—but the future doesn't actually exist, even though we've been taught that it does. There is no such thing as the future. This is a quantum physics concept that is difficult for some people to grasp, but stay with me.

The only reality you experience is this moment, a series of moments we call "now" (now . . . now . . . now . . .). If you understand that life is not made of the space and time that we witness, such as a past, present, and future, but rather of a series of "now" moments that stand in their own space, then there is no future because the present is continuous. *A Course in Miracles* says:

> Fear is not of the present, but only of the past and future, which do not exist. There is no fear in the present when each instant stands clear and separated from the past, without its shadow reaching out into the future . . . And the present extends forever.

If there is no fear in the present moment and the present extends forever, then that means that fear cannot exist. It is only in your mind, and it has been planted there by the ego.

Whenever I've been gripped with fear, I've made a point to get out of the trap of the perceived future pain and plant myself right in the present moment. For me, fear usually creeps up at three o'clock in the morning, so I'm usually in bed.

This is what I do to get back into the present moment. I ask myself to focus on what is real, right in this present moment, and really be in the moment. I use my senses to notice the softness of the pillow, the warmth of the blanket over me, the sound of my husband quietly sleeping next to me. I look at the tree branches right outside my window. I listen for the wind outside. I think about my three children in their beds. I focus my attention on the present moment and the fact that in this moment, I am safe. Everything is good in this moment. And then in this moment, and then in this moment . . . When I do this, I keep myself in the present moment, in which fear cannot exist. The fear is banished.

When you live in the present moment, the ego cannot survive. In fact, gratitude and fear cannot occupy the same space in time, so the more you stay in gratitude in a given moment, the more you expel the fear. This is a surprisingly easy exercise, and it's a spiritual practice at the same time because being in the present moment means you are connected with your source. The more present you are and the more grateful you are, the more you banish the fear that was just gripping you. You align with God.

61. Based on faith, not fear

"Fear knocked at the door. Faith answered.
And lo, no one was there."

—AUTHOR UNKNOWN

The opposite of love is not hate. It's actually fear.

Of all the emotions on the scale of human emotions, the lowest is fear. Not only does it make you retreat to playing small and not reaching your goals or your potential but if you fall for it and put your attention on what you fear, you'll actually manifest the exact thing you fear. Being in fear creates more fear.

Whatever you put your intense attention and focus on is what you will attract in your life. That's rule number one in manifestation. This is good when you're feeling good about manifesting something you want. But when it comes to being afraid that something bad is going to happen, then the more you put your energy into thinking about that, the more you are hastening its arrival in your life.

So the key is to not let yourself be afraid.

How you feel in a particular moment is your choice. To get out of fear, you can change how you feel in each moment, away from fear and into something that feels better. Switch from being consumed with fear (or worry or doubt) and flip right into faith and trust, appreciation and gratitude. It may seem difficult at first, but it's actually pretty simple, and it's very effective.

Love, faith, trust, and gratitude are the highest-frequency vibrations in the universe. They are at the opposite end of the spectrum from fear. When you are feeling any of these, it is impossible to feel fear, making it impossible to attract the thing you fear.

Esther and Jerry Hicks wrote about the list of 22 emotions in their remarkable book, *Ask and It Is Given*. I have used this list for many years and prominently display it in my office and my home. It is a constant reminder that you are ultimately in charge of your life because you are in charge of your feelings and emotions. You'll notice that some emotions are grouped together even though they are different. This is because they share the same frequency.

If you often feel one of the first seven emotions, then you are almost always attracting what you want in your life.

1. Joy/Appreciation/Empowered/Freedom/Love
2. Passion
3. Enthusiasm/Eagerness/Happiness
4. Positive Expectation/Belief
5. Optimism
6. Hopefulness
7. Contentment

When you find yourself feeling any combination of the remaining 15 emotions, you are most likely repelling what you want in your life, and struggling, wondering what's not working.

8. Boredom
9. Pessimism
10. Frustration/Irritation/Impatience

11. Overwhelment

12. Disappointment

13. Doubt

14. Worry

15. Blame

16. Discouragement

17. Anger

18. Revenge

19. Hatred/Rage

20. Jealousy

21. Insecurity/Guilt/Unworthiness

22. Fear/Grief/Depression/Despair/
    Powerlessness

Notice that fear is the last and lowest of the 22 emotions. You cannot get lower than fear, grief, depression, despair, and powerlessness. In fact, that's exactly what fear is—powerlessness. That's what the ego wants for you. That's how the ego keeps you under its thumb.

On the flip side, if you continually find yourself in a place of gratitude, appreciation, faith, and trust, the highest vibrational frequencies you can be feeling, you bypass the ego and its trappings. You are filled with confidence that anything is possible, because anything is when you have faith.

So how do you flip the switch? How do you transition from the lowest to the highest frequency? For me, the key has been to focus on faith and feeling good. If I'm sensing the grip of fear in my life, usually when I'm attempting something big and bold that will have a great impact on my life and the lives of others, my immediate reaction is to recognize that this fear is not real.

Let me give you an example of something that happened not too long ago. With the arrival of our third child, Derek and I felt that we were outgrowing our house. We wanted to move to a home in the same neighborhood that had at least five bedrooms. We didn't know of any houses that matched these specifications, but we put out the intention that if one was available, it would come on the market at just the right time.

Just a few months after we set our intention, a house no one would have imagined being sold came on the market. It was bigger than we had anticipated and right in our neighborhood. I saw this house as a once-in-a-lifetime opportunity. It was an unusual property because it had not originally been designed to be a residence, and not everyone who walked through it shared the vision we had. Yet, deep in our hearts, we knew that we wanted this house and that it was meant to be ours.

As we started the purchasing process, the fact that it was an unusual style of property created many unexpected obstacles and delays. Ultimately, its uniqueness caused concerns about how we would afford it, despite the fact that we were doing well financially. These fears translated into self-doubt about whether we belonged in that kind of house, concerns that it would rock the boat in our relationship, and that living there would invite criticism from people we knew.

Then came a defining moment in our journey. The seller gave us an ultimatum of sorts that would have had financial implications if we couldn't get a particular type of mortgage. This was risky. Everyone advised us to really weigh the consequences, which were substantial. We had 24 hours to make a decision on whether we would go ahead with the process or forgo our dream house.

With so little time, I sat down at the dining room table and made a simple pros-and-cons list with Derek and our real estate agent. The list of pros was long. The list of cons was short but frightening. While Derek and the real estate agent were discussing our options in the kitchen, I sat at the table for quite some time. Pros versus cons were both weighing very heavily and with considerable implications either way.

I stared at the lists for some time, and then clarity washed over me. I called out to them excitedly, "Wooohooo! I figured it out! We're buying the house!"

They both rushed into the dining room and looked at me in puzzlement, wondering how I'd managed to sort out something that seemed so complicated. I showed them the simple fact that the left column (pros) was really based on faith and wanting an even richer, fuller, more abundant life. The right column (cons) was all based on fear of losing a considerable amount of money if things didn't turn out the way we wanted. It was basically faith versus fear, God versus ego.

I said to them that, since Derek and I are both spiritual people, we believe in the power of faith. "We make decisions based on faith, not from fear. Let's get this house." I understood that faith is God wanting the best for us, and fear is our wicked ego, trying to keep us playing small, not moving from the status quo.

So we went for it and agreed to the seller's conditions. From that day, Derek and I stayed in faith, even when confronted with worry, doubt, and fear.

Lo and behold, we did it. The right solutions and resources, ones I'd never heard existed, manifested themselves. Everything fell into place, and the rest is history. We stayed in faith and said yes to the opportunities that came, even when they didn't make sense at first. We are now proud owners of this beautiful property, having survived an intense process I'm not sure most people would have withstood.

How do you eliminate fear from your own life? Make decisions from faith, not fear. Once you've made the decision to go ahead, do whatever it takes to stay in faith at all times. God works miracles for you when you stay in faith. Trusting the universe means that you understand that your resolve may be tested, but you are stronger than ego.

Now, I'm not suggesting you make foolish financial decisions. Don't. We had done our due diligence and had the means to afford this house.

What I do suggest is that you read books on developing faith. Surround yourself with positive people. Stay away from people who complain, blame, and whine (at least for a short while). Stop watching news programs and reading newspapers that have a fear-based angle. Watch videos or movies that inspire faith. Talk to friends who are faithful and positive. Read or watch anything that keeps you in the present moment. Make a long list of things you are grateful for. Go on a gratitude walk with a child, pointing out things that look nice or that you're grateful for. Spend more time with children—they love being in the moment.

Most important, stay in a place of positive expectation, knowing that the opportunities for what you want will be given to you, just when you need them, if you stay in faith. They always will.

If you'd like a copy of the positive expectation mantra I hang in my home and office, you can download one at www.EmbraceYourMagnificence.com/resources.

62. The ultimate parachute

"Nothing splendid has ever been achieved except by those who dared believe that something inside of them was superior to circumstance."

—BRUCE BARTON

The secret ingredient to pushing through fear is courage supported by faith. Having courage means taking action, despite the intense fear that comes along with taking that action. It means feeling the fear and walking right into it anyway. It is acting in spite of the gripping fear.

I have found that the only way to get beyond the fear is with courage, when it is supported by faith. In fact, courage comes from faith, from surrendering and trusting that all is well.

Imagine jumping off a cliff. The fear is that certain death will follow, and you will not do it. But if you were given a parachute, then even though some fear might still be there, you would be more likely to have the courage to jump off that cliff, knowing that all would be well.

The same is true for life. If you have something that you want to do that scares you (the equivalent of jumping off a cliff), you will not do it until you have faith that it will indeed work out (your parachute). The parachute will give you the courage to do it, knowing all is well.

Faith is your parachute. God is your parachute. You will be protected if you believe.

Having deep faith and trust in the universe, believing that you will be taken care of, surrendering to the guidance, and expecting miracles: this is what will give you the courage to do anything you want in life and succeed at it.

Most people avoid discomfort like the plague. Once you decide to go for something and you actually walk into your fear, you will realize that the act of walking into it is never as bad as you feared. In fact, the gripping fear feels worse than the actual act of walking into it.

Make a commitment to change your life for the better by taking more action, not falling prey to fear. Surrender to trust and faith, knowing you are taken care of. Be vigilant about doing battle with the false fear.

Having faith means believing in something, even if the evidence of it is not right in front of you at the moment. It is about being superstubborn about your positive expectation. Even one ounce of doubt can sabotage you, because doubt leads to worry, worry leads to fear, fear leads to blame and resentment, and blame and resentment lead to giving up.

This is one of the most important battles you'll ever fight in your life.

The battle with fear is always strongest when you reach for bigger and bigger change. When you can successfully walk into it, you disarm the ego. Like giving birth, it's a temporary discomfort that sometimes feels unbearable, but it's short-lived. When you are past it, the greatest treasure awaits you.

Whenever you feel gripping fear about taking a step forward, know that you are on the right track. This is the ego signaling you that you are on the verge of great evolution. Over time, this becomes a game you recognize and want to play, because you know the discomfort of the fear is short-lived and rich rewards are on their way if you stay in courage and faith. Whenever there is a breakdown or a fear, you can observe the ego at work and say to yourself, "Oh, I must be on the verge of another big breakthrough! Okay, then, bring it on!"

63. The trickeries of resistance

"Self-sabotage is when you say you want something and then go about making sure it doesn't happen."

—ALYCE P. CORNYN-SELBY

The enemy is the thought that comes into your head that says, *I know I should do it, but I don't feel like it.* Resistance is doing the thing that you know you should not do, or not doing the thing you know you should be doing. It is giving in to temptation even though you've made a promise to yourself not to. It is giving in to instant gratification, a momentary fall from your commitment.

Even though you've committed yourself to doing something that will bring you the fulfillment and richness of life that you desire, you do its opposite. You make a promise to yourself, and then you get tempted by the voice inside that says it's okay to not do it, that you can start tomorrow.

Resistance is the enemy. It is another tool of the ego, prompting you to do the opposite of what you really want to do. It keeps you small and takes you down unless you resist it.

The ego hates it when you decide to run on the treadmill or choose a green smoothie in the morning rather than your usual bacon, egg, and cheese sandwich. The ego hates it when you actually call that prospective client as soon as they reach out to you or write that article you've been putting off writing. It senses that you are saying yes to spirit and to evolution, rather than to the smallness that it wants for you.

Resistance has been one of the most insidious things I've ever dealt with. It continually contributed to my once low self-esteem and feelings of inadequacy about myself, my weight, my past relationships, and many things in my life. It is the basis for procrastination, for making choices your intuition tells you not to make. It has shown up for me on a daily basis for most of my life.

Saying yes to these nagging impulses can cause momentary pleasure or relief, but it does not provide ongoing pleasure. The momentary pleasure always fizzles out and is replaced with guilt and regret, disappointment and depression. This causes us to feel bad about ourselves for having given in, which then makes us feel like we have no control of our own lives, creating a feeling of being somehow flawed and helpless and hopeless.

This is where self-discipline comes in. The word *discipline* used to make me cringe. I've never thought I was someone who was disciplined. In fact, I considered myself someone who didn't have a lot of self-control in many parts of my life. But after more than 40 years of regrets and feeling like I was inadequate and, on the flip side, feeling a huge sense of accomplishment and self-confidence when I did the thing that I was supposed to do, I've realized there is no other way. Self-discipline is a slow process, but it's one that I am embracing little by little, because self-discipline brings you feelings of self-worth and happiness.

In the end, the pain of regret and disappointment and the self-beating-up that happen after you surrender to the ego's temptations are much greater than the momentary discomfort that comes from ignoring the resistance and doing the right thing anyway.

Your ability to resist resistance itself becomes more refined as you continue to do it. It's like a spiritual practice; it must be done every day and in every way. You will become stronger and stronger in this process the longer you do it.

64. The difference between a winner and a whiner

"When you're interested, you do what's convenient;
when you're committed, you do whatever it takes."

—JOHN ASSARAF

It's fascinating to see people ask for change in their lives. When they are presented with the opportunity that will create that change, many people say no to it. They beg for a change, for an increase in the number of clients they have or an improvement in their health, and when the way for that to happen is delivered, they decline it, still complaining about the fact that they're in the same position that they were in before.

One of the ways we sabotage ourselves and get in our own way of living a richer, fuller, more abundant life is by using excuses for not doing something. Remember, when you ask, the universe delivers the way for you to accomplish, in the form of an opportunity. When that opportunity lands in your lap, recognize it as a sign and take action on it.

But most people who aren't living the life they want make excuses for not saying yes to the opportunity. The biggest excuses I hear in my business are:

"I don't have enough money to do that."

"I don't have enough time to do that."

"I'm too busy to do that," or "I'm already busy that day."

"I don't want to travel."

"I can't leave my children."

"I can't leave my husband/job/pet/ailing parents."

"I'm too old/young to do that."

"It's not really what I want after all."

These are all ways that you stop the flow of abundance. You have asked, the universe has provided, and now you are saying no to that opportunity. Ultimately, you are saying no to the thing you previously said you wanted.

Imagine that I called you and said that you just inherited $100,000 in cash from your great-aunt Matilda, that it was legitimately yours, and that there was no downside or repercussions to you having it. In fact, this money was legally yours and all you had to do was fly to the other side of the world, escorted by a trusted police officer, in order to collect it. Would you say to me, "I don't have the money to do that" or "I don't have the time" or "I'm too busy, and, besides, I don't like to travel"? Most people wouldn't. They would find a way, find the time, find the money for the flight. They would find childcare or bring the kids along. They would do whatever it took, because the reward would be greater than the effort.

And yet these are the same excuses you sometimes use to say no to the opportunities that come in. Logically, it doesn't make sense that you wouldn't say yes to an opportunity you asked for. But it's easy to reject the opportunity by using excuses, because it's more convenient to stay in your comfort zone than to do whatever it takes.

That's the difference between a winner and a whiner. The winner is the one who takes a no-excuses approach to life, saying yes to the right opportunities. The whiner will say no to the opportunities that show up, not take action, and then complain that they are still struggling.

Sometimes I've pointed out to one of my students that he or she is using an excuse not to take action, and the reply has been, "No, Fabienne, it's not an excuse. I've got a good reason. There's a family reunion that weekend."

Beware of how you turn excuses into "reasons" for not doing something. They're the same thing. You can live a life of excuses, or you can live a life you love. Which do you want?

Often the question I get is, "Which of all the opportunities should I say yes to? There are just so many!" My simple method for selecting opportunities I will take action on is asking myself the following questions:

- What is the goal I want to accomplish?

- What is the biggest difference I will experience by accomplishing this goal?

- Will this opportunity get me significantly closer to my goal?

- What is the best-case scenario that will occur if I take action on this opportunity?

- What is the worst-case scenario if I don't take action on this opportunity?

If the opportunity feels like it's something I should definitely do because it will get me closer to my goal, then I do it, without excuses. If not, then I don't.

65. The three-bagger

"Nothing is impossible to a willing heart."

— PROVERB

Big players, top money earners, and people who love their lives are people who've decided to make their goals and dreams happen, regardless of the effort required. For them, convenience is not an option. They are inherently lazy, too, just as we all are to some degree, but their commitment to their dream is bigger than the commitment to "I don't feel like it."

You must be willing to do what it takes to create the life you want. Willingness is everything. Imagine that you are an immigrant, that you don't have the luxuries of convenience, but your dream is big. When that's the case, you do whatever it takes. I've met people who were doctors in their countries of origin, but in America they wash dishes, babysit, or clean houses as temporary stepping-stones to their dreams, because they so badly want to live here. I've met people who quit highly successful corporate jobs to become unpaid apprentices so they could learn a new trade, something they love.

For all these people, the commitment to making things different and the willingness to do whatever it takes to achieve that difference were stronger than the inconvenience or discomfort that came with the dream. And yet many others get stopped from doing what it takes because of their sense of entitlement, a feeling that they are owed something without having to put in the work.

Consider the person at the supermarket who bags your groceries. Have you ever seen someone do this one bag at a time, taking his time, slowing things down when you're in a hurry? That's the person I call the one-bagger. Then there's the person who's got two bags lined up, steadily putting your items in both bags at the same time; this two-bagger is moving things along much faster.

Rarely do we ever see the three-bagger, the person who is willing to do things better, faster, more efficiently, without any sense of entitlement, and with a smile and a great attitude.

Which of these three people do you think will be given a raise first? Which will be promoted? Which will end up being more successful in life? Which would you hire if it were your company? Yes, the answer is obvious. It's the three-bagger.

The ironic thing is the one-bagger is the one who will be cranky and complain that he didn't get a raise.

He'll be resentful that he's stuck in the same job (or has lost his job) and isn't making much money. The one-bagger will blame the company, blame the system, blame the economy, and resent successful people. But all the one-bagger had to do was model himself after the three-bagger. He had to be willing to do a little bit more, give a little bit more, and then he would have gained the same results and advantages as the three-bagger. Rewards don't come from entitlement. Everything must be earned.

Where are you being a one-bagger or even a two-bagger in your life? What have you not been willing to do in the past? How will you change that to reach your potential?

Let others be satisfied with playing a small game. Be the one to choose a different path. Be the one to play a much bigger game. Your purpose here on earth is too big for excuses, resistance, and unwillingness. Do whatever it takes. The time is now.

Chapter 11

Be in the Moment

66. Live life like you mean it

"One of the secrets of a happy life is continuous small treats."

—IRIS MURDOCH

Too many people live to work instead of working to live. Perhaps it's because I was raised in France, where the pleasures of the senses are celebrated, but I feel that we are too focused on accumulation rather than appreciation and lingering. You've been made to feel guilty if you don't work into the night after putting the kids to bed, and this is depleting you.

Yes, I believe in working hard and doing what it takes. But if you can't enjoy the fruits of your labor, then what's the point of all the hard work? You must take time to enjoy and celebrate your accomplishments. You must take time to be still and have pleasure in your life. Otherwise, you become a robot.

Enjoy every moment and live life in each moment. Living well is transformative, and it doesn't have to cost any money. Living well means enjoying your food and reveling in your comfort. Take time off. Book a two-day "stay-close-to-home" vacation with your spouse. Surround yourself with beautiful things and spend time doing the things that make you happy.

It means putting yourself at the top of the list and taking time to savor the sensual pleasures of life: fresh flowers, a brisk walk outside, a favorite meal, music, reading by a crackling fire, laughing with friends, a quiet afternoon with your kids, or date night with your spouse.

Create some standards and boundaries in your life about how you want to live. If you were a billionaire and could create the ideal life, how would you enjoy your days? What would you do with your weekends? How would you spend your time? Who would you spend it with?

Make this list right now, without any reservations. Just focus on what you enjoy most in life. If that's difficult for you, make a list of what you don't enjoy first, and then flip it around. Once you've done that, create a list of standards, or new ways you want to live. For example, if you find yourself working into the night, constantly checking your e-mail, and doing work on weekends, then create a new standard that you will shut down the computer by 6:30 each night and that weekends are work-free.

Yes, this can be difficult at first, especially when you've been trained that nothing is more important than getting items checked off the to-do list. But nothing is more important than creating these standards, because if you don't do this for yourself, you won't have any energy to give to anything else you enjoy. You will deplete yourself over time. If you don't refill the oil lamp, there will be no light left for you to shine and illuminate others.

Make these simple pleasures a priority. Yes, your to-do list is a mile long, but no small children will ever be harmed if you carry over a part of your to-do list to the next day. This is not procrastination or resistance. It's about focusing on the three most important things that need to get done to reach your goals for that day, and then giving yourself permission not to work yourself into the ground. Rather, enjoy yourself.

There must be a balance. Sometimes that means saying no to something big or pacing it out so that your life is not one-sided. If you don't, you will become a prisoner in your own life. You will feel trapped, unable to get off the track.

Life can be short. It could all end tomorrow. Stop being robotic about life. Put a pause button on going through the motions and not taking in all the real moments. Make every moment count.

67. The traps of distraction

"Realize deeply that the present moment is all you ever have. Make the Now the primary focus of your life."

—ECKHART TOLLE

Focus on one thing and one thing only. When you are doing something, be totally present to that one thing. We are taught that multitasking is being efficient, but I believe that it is a major obstacle—not only to productivity but to happiness. When we do too many things at once, we dilute our focus, get distracted, and actually delay the results from all the tasks we are working on.

Yes, people pride themselves on being able to write an article, be on Facebook, talk on the phone, and make dinner at the same time, but nothing good can come out of taking yourself out of the moment and constantly interrupting one thing to switch to another. In fact, each time that you switch from one thing to another, you must spend extra time getting reacquainted with the new task and you delay the outcome.

Avoid the traps of distraction by focusing on one thing and one thing only until completion. Allow yourself to complete that task before moving on to the next thing.

When my husband first joined me in my business, he didn't realize that I worked this way. He would come to my office with a "quick" question or a task for me, the way someone would just drop by a colleague's cubicle in a corporation.

The thing is there is no such thing as a "quick" question, and his task would have taken my focus off the task I was working on. At first, I would ask, "Is it urgent?" When he said no, I'd say, "Okay. I'm focused now. Let me finish this task at hand and I'll reach out to you." This was surprising to him at first, and for many people I've worked with, it has initially seemed like I was being rude. But I have found that when you put yourself in an uninterrupted flow, you can produce much more in less time than if you stop and start incessantly.

Again, this is about setting boundaries and educating people around you. Tell them that you prefer to finish what you're working on and then you'll be available to them. At other times, you must set boundaries with yourself, to keep yourself on task and avoid distractions—whether it's e-mail, the Internet, the phone, or any other screen that is grabbing your attention.

Children are often on the losing end of multitasking. I call this the just-one-more-e-mail-honey-and-Mommy-will-be-right-there syndrome. Many parents think it's okay if they are physically with their children while their attention is on a screen. I have done this many times, and it is still tempting. Yet I've found that when I do this, I cheat my children and make them feel as if they don't matter.

Many self-employed people who work from home like I have divide their limited attention between their work and their kids, constantly switching from a work task to paying attention to the child. I've concluded that this is a losing proposition for both the business and the child. You cheat your business by not being fully focused on the task at hand and not giving it your all. More important, you cheat your children by not being fully engaged, which can affect their self-esteem down the road.

The solution for me has been to compartmentalize different areas of my life and block out time for each thing. When I work from home, my children know that Mommy's working; it's "Mommy's work time." And when I'm free, it's absolutely family time.

In fact, when my kids were younger and before we had offices outside the home, I drew a sign on a sheet of printer paper. One side had a smiley face with the words "Mommy is free," and the other side had a sad face with the words "Mommy is busy." The one child who could read was able to immediately see that I was free. The other could determine my availability by looking at the face. It worked for years.

My children were fine with me working at home (with a babysitter, of course) because when my work was done at 5:30 and it became family time, work was not allowed to creep in at all. I made a commitment to them, and I stuck with it. They could look forward to family time knowing that I wouldn't cheat them by looking at e-mail or doing paperwork.

Obviously, there is always the rare occasion when things need to get done and cannot wait for the next day. But the boundaries are pretty strict with me. It's allowed me to really be in the moment, fully focused on my work when I need to be and fully able to enjoy each moment with my husband and children, making them feel significant.

68. Grapefruit moments

"Anything worth doing is worth doing slowly."

— MAE WEST

The happiest times in your life will always be when you are totally present to something or someone. When you are present, you are focused, intentional, purposeful, and connected to your source. You are filled with peace. Stillness overcomes you. Beauty surrounds you. Nothing else can get in the way.

This is especially true of spending time with the people you love. So many times, wrapped up in the hectic schedule of daily life, we move through our day robotically, going through the motions, forgetting that each moment is slipping through our hands unless we stop to notice it and the people who are in it with us.

Cherish every moment with those you love as if it were the very last one. Tell them you love them every single day. Never leave the house without giving them a kiss, even if you're just running to the store. Let your eyes light up when your loved ones walk through the doorway. Let yourself run to them, even if you're just picking up your kids at the bus stop. Always make the people in your life feel significant. Make everyone feel significant, no matter who they are.

You will find the greatest joy when you dive into the eyes of a person you love and keep that gaze filled with all the love you can conjure. Smile with your eyes. Let yourself linger and love that particular moment, and then the next, and then the next. When you are present and in the moment, you experience no fear, only bliss.

I call these the "grapefruit moments" in my family. Many years ago, Derek and I were sitting at the kitchen table on a Saturday morning, sharing a grapefruit with our little kids. One bite of grapefruit for Mommy, one for our child, one for Daddy, and so on. We were completely present and in the moment. No TV, no distractions, nothing but pure presence, smiling at how sweet it was. We didn't even need to talk. We just stayed in the moment, enjoying every second of it. Nothing could get in the way. It was joy, it was bliss, and it was one of those moments you remember forever.

I strive to measure my life by how many grapefruit moments I can have. The more of them I experience, the more blissful I am, the more abundant I feel, and the more I love my life.

Chapter 12

Embrace Your Magnificence

69. Rock the boat

"I do not fear . . . I was born to do this."

—JOAN OF ARC

To fully live up to your calling and live a life that is rich, full, and abundant, your greatest challenge is to be absolutely, totally true to yourself. You must believe in yourself, loving yourself warts and all. You must accept yourself as a child of God, accept your purpose, have compassion for yourself, and, most important, express fully who you are and what you believe. You must share all that is you, without regard for what others think or how they will react to it, no matter what the consequences.

To fully express yourself, you must set aside any tendency to put on a mask. Instead, tear down the walls that separate you and your truth from the world. The ways in which you haven't been authentic and any false pretenses must stop. This is so important that I urge you to see it as going into battle in the same way Joan of Arc went into each battle—with courage, conviction, faith, perseverance, and fierce determination.

You've succumbed to and previously accepted some false beliefs about yourself and your capabilities. These false beliefs come from family, religion, teachers, and society, and they are not true. Accepting them causes a loss of your sense of self and disconnects you from yourself and your true and just power.

At the same time, your sense of the importance of what you are being called to do also generates a level of fear and anxiety deep inside. The anxiety is the voice of your soul wishing to be freed into full expression. It is battling against the fear of what might happen if you do so. The "what might happen if I am really myself" is a fear that is primal and feels dangerous. The fear of being rejected, cast out from the tribe, is a fear of great proportions, and it feels like the fear of death.

Most people don't even know that this fear exists and even fewer are determined to face it. Instead, they allow this fear to guide their decisions and determine their choices, while they create a false front and stay numb.

For a long time, I too stayed numb and hid from my own truth and purpose. I was afraid of how big it is. I was afraid to rock the boat. My calling here is to be a spiritual teacher and healer in the world community. I believe deep in my heart that the time is now for light-workers to gather their strength and heal the world. I am here to help others awaken to their own callings and potentials for greatness. I am here to help them step into it with courage and faith, taking a no-excuses approach to playing a much bigger game. That is my "big why" and my mission here, the thing that gives me purpose and scares me at the same time.

The fear of it all sometimes makes me want to hide, numb out, and go into avoidance and denial. It's easy to slip into thoughts that go against your reason for being here.

"It's too hard."

"There's too much to do."

"It's an overwhelming task. I can't possibly do this on my own."

"I don't have what it takes."

"I don't know enough."

"I'm not strong enough."

"I'm scared."

"What if they think I'm crazy and reject me?"

Sometimes I cry about this.

But then the calling is stronger than me, and I know I have no choice but to get my message out there and help as many people as I can. I help them wake up to their potentials and play a much bigger game in service to others, no matter what my ego says and no matter what the fear is.

You too must face the fear and walk right into it. With your bravery and courage, you will face these fears.

One thing to remember is that you will sometimes want to slip into avoidance and denial. You will want to forget that you're here for something big. But you must refrain from any activities that you may currently indulge in that ease or muffle the fear. You must set aside any tendency to ease your anxiety. Feel the anxiety, feel the fear, feel them fully—and then take action in spite of the fears. Your purpose here is that important.

70. You are indeed very, very useful

"Let others lead small lives, but not you."

—JIM ROHN

Embrace what is true about yourself: you are rare and precious, very brave and strong. You are capable of greatness bigger than you can imagine, whether you see this right now or not. There is no other like you. You are magnificent, here to influence lives and shift the world in your own way. Your actions will reverberate like ripples in a placid lake, touching more people's lives than you can imagine and in a way that no one else could. Your purpose for being here is much, much bigger than you think. God created you, and God doesn't play small, especially when He made you. You are here to manifest change, and not just on a small level.

With every person you meet or who hears about you, you will make a mark, and this will affect them and those they know. This will create an untold ripple effect that will be passed on to others, even if they don't realize it, even if you don't realize it. In fact, you'll never really know the magnitude of your effect on people, but please don't underestimate it.

If you have been looking for the meaning behind everything you've experienced so far—the good, the not so good, and the painful—this is why you experienced it. Everything was for a reason; every experience was a piece of the puzzle that is you, a stitch in your quilt. Your life so far has been your training course in getting you to this point, in making you someone who is here to make a difference in the world and be a catalyst for others.

You were created to exact specifications for a very specific purpose. It's time for you to awaken to that calling, to turn your pain and experiences around and use them to be of service to others, to help others move across their own thresholds into their own magnificence so that they too can make a difference and live a fuller, richer, more abundant life.

The time is now. This is why it's important for you to get out of the way by changing how small you perceive yourself to be, awakening to the magnificent work that you are meant to do here on earth.

71. Between a rock and a hard place

"Truth, like gold, is to be obtained not by its growth, but by washing away from it all that is not gold."

—LEO TOLSTOY

You are magnificent. Yet you've also been taught some things that are not true about yourself, and these have been getting in the way of you stepping into your calling and fulfilling your greatness. You've been made to feel substandard, that you are not good enough, that you don't have what it takes, that you don't know enough or aren't equipped to do great things. You've been made to believe that you are small and unimportant, that your opinion doesn't matter, that you belong to a group of people who don't matter, and that you are somehow less valuable than others.

You have somehow accepted these false beliefs on a subconscious level. They are clashing and creating a chaotic vibration within you. One side (led by your higher self and spirit) tells you that you are magnificent and here for great things; the other side of you (led by ego and false beliefs) tells you that you are somehow less than others and that your opinions don't matter.

The false beliefs you've been given about how small you are and how little your importance is here on earth create your greatest pain. It's a primordial pain; it's visceral and lodged deep inside. Acting on a subconscious level, your belief of these things that are untrue about you chips away at and diminishes the truth about you, making you feel less potent about your usefulness in the world.

That is the rock. Then there is the hard place.

The hard place contains your strength and your courage. It contains great faith in universal beliefs and principles. The hard place holds the belief that you are precious and perfect and glorious. The hard place states that you must be determined to become your true self, warts and all, in order to heal the pain of false beliefs about yourself. The hard place states that you are perfect in the eyes of all there is, and that you have the right and the true responsibility to be your authentic, glorious, most magnificent self.

Often, you feel stuck between the rock and the hard place.

72. The tug-of-war inside

"Life is a sum of all your choices."

—ALBERT CAMUS

In between the rock and the hard place is a place of deep choice that will determine your destiny and the destiny of many others. It is a place of free will where you are pulled by the forces calling you to give up trying to be great and instead succumb to the false beliefs that you are not so special after all, to wither into being small and hopeless and helpless.

The counterpull calls you to gather your strength, deny your smallness, and grab hold of the truth of your incredible wonderfulness, your vast love, your deep compassion, and your purpose as a spiritual warrior in service to the world.

This place exists and is reflected in all great myths and metaphors. It is the place where the smallness of the single soul must struggle and must come in the final hour to call out for help, to receive the grace of God. This is the place, if you choose it, where the old small self will be extinguished, to be replaced by the transformed you, the one who no longer sees the world through the small eyes of the ego self but sees instead the vast potency and promise of a world that is healed.

When you realize that you are here to be of service and how big the shift is that you are on this planet to make; when you step in with courage, knowing that the universe, spirit, source, all that is, God is walking right beside you; when you begin to do your work here—you will no longer be concerned about money, power, and fame. You will be concerned only with your absolute loyalty in service to others. That's when you will be handsomely rewarded by all these external things.

Those who are of service get rewarded in the biggest way. The more value you bring to the world, using your unique talents, purpose, experiences, knowledge, skills, and intuition, the more you will be rewarded with riches, fulfillment, meaning, and fame. It is when you are focused on service rather than on accumulation and are no longer concerned about things that they will come to you. When you embrace your magnificence and step into your purpose here on earth is precisely when you will live a richer, fuller, and more abundant life.

"There is only one time when it is essential to awaken. That time is now."

—BUDDHA

Embrace your magnificence. Step in.
Say yes. Go forth. Have faith.
I believe in you. I love you.

ABOUT THE AUTHOR

Fabienne Fredrickson is an inspirational mentor to thousands of clients worldwide, an author, international speaker and founder of The Client Attraction Business School™ and ClientAttraction.com, ranked repeatedly by *Inc.* magazine as one of America's fastest growing private companies and recipient of the 2013 Stevie® Award for Entrepreneur of the Year.

As one of the most influential and highly acclaimed success mind-set speakers and mentors in the world, Fabienne believes in the capacity for each and every person to become the full expression of their purpose here on earth by taking a no-excuses approach to growing within and having a willingness to 'play a bigger game'. Her mind-set teachings, born from Fabienne's own personal experiences and challenges and once intended for entrepreneurs, are now embraced by women all around the world who seek a catalyst for their personal and professional growth and to live a life they love.

www.clientattraction.com

A PERSONAL MESSAGE FROM FABIENNE

I hope with all my heart that this book has inspired you and that the words and lessons within these pages will act as a catalyst in your life, to help you live a fuller, richer, more abundant life. If you'd like access to more resources for deeper learning or to find out about attending a live Embrace Your Magnificence event, please visit www.EmbraceYourMagnificence.com.

Now that you've read each page and taken in the stories and suggestions, perhaps you'll help me spread the word by letting your heart guide you to think of other women in your life who would benefit from these lessons and invite them to go on this journey with us. I deeply believe that the core of this message is universal and that it has the power and potential to change a person's life, and then the lives of countless others as a result.

To that end, if you feel called to help me spread the word to friends, family, your networks, or your organization, I invite you to contact us via info@EmbraceYour Magnificence.com for bulk book purchase requests, as well as requests to speak for your organization. This is a message that must be shared.

If you own a business and are interested in finding out more about attracting more clients, making more money, and multiplying your business with authenticity, integrity, and love, please visit www.ClientAttraction.com to discover how The Client Attraction Business School™ can help you achieve that, as well as request a free audio CD entitled *How to Attract All the Clients You Need.*

Thank you for being in my life.

Hay House Titles of Related Interest

YOU CAN HEAL YOUR LIFE, the movie,
starring Louise Hay & Friends
(available as a 1-DVD program and an expanded 2-DVD set)
Watch the trailer at: www.LouiseHayMovie.com

THE SHIFT, the movie, starring Dr Wayne W. Dyer
(available as a 1-DVD program and an expanded 2-DVD set)
Watch the trailer at: www.DyerMovie.com

ASK AND IT IS GIVEN: Learning to Manifest Your Desires,
by Esther and Jerry Hicks

*E-SQUARED: Nine Do-It-Yourself Energy Experiments That Prove
Your Thoughts Create Your Reality,* by Pam Grout

STOP THE EXCUSES!: How to Change Lifelong Thoughts,
by Dr Wayne W. Dyer

WISHES FULFILLED: Mastering the Art of Manifesting,
by Dr Wayne W. Dyer

YOU CAN CREATE AN EXCEPTIONAL LIFE, by Louise Hay
and Cheryl Richardson

All of the above are available at your local bookstore,
or may be ordered by contacting Hay House (see next page).

We hope you enjoyed this Hay House book. If you'd like to receive our online catalogue featuring additional information on Hay House books and products, or if you'd like to find out more about the Hay Foundation, please contact:

Hay House UK, Ltd., Astley House, 33 Notting Hill Gate, London W11 3JQ
Phone: 0-20-3675-2450 • *Fax:* 0-20-3675-2451
www.hayhouse.co.uk • www.hayfoundation.org

Published and distributed in Australia by:
Hay House Australia Pty. Ltd., 18/36 Ralph St., Alexandria NSW 2015
Phone: 612-9669-4299 • *Fax:* 612-9669-4144 • www.hayhouse.com.au

Published and distributed in the United States by:
Hay House, Inc., P.O. Box 5100, Carlsbad, CA 92018-5100
Phone: (760) 431-7695 or (800) 654-5126
Fax: (760) 431-6948 or (800) 650-5115
www.hayhouse.com®

Published and distributed in the Republic of South Africa by:
Hay House SA (Pty), Ltd., P.O. Box 990, Witkoppen 2068
Phone/Fax: 27-11-467-8904 • www.hayhouse.co.za

Published in India by: Hay House Publishers India,
Muskaan Complex, Plot No. 3, B-2, Vasant Kunj, New Delhi 110 070
Phone: 91-11-4176-1620 • *Fax:* 91-11-4176-1630 • www.hayhouse.co.in

Distributed in Canada by: Raincoast Books,
2440 Viking Way, Richmond, B.C. V6V 1N2
Phone: 1-800-663-5714 • *Fax:* 1-800-565-3770 • www.raincoast.com

Take Your Soul on a Vacation

Visit www.HealYourLife.com® to regroup, recharge,
and reconnect with your own magnificence.
Featuring blogs, mind-body-spirit news, and
life-changing wisdom from Louise Hay and friends.

Visit www.HealYourLife.com today!